Woman In Love

BY KATIE HARTFIEL

Hearts United

Hearts United

PO Box 6947
Katy, TX 77491

www.womaninlove.org

Cover Design: Saint Louis Creative

To My Girls: May Each of You Always
Be a Woman In Love
&
To The Blessed Mother: The First
Woman In Love

Acknowledgements

I cannot begin to offer thanks without first thanking the one who captured my heart and transformed me into a Woman in Love. All glory goes to the Lord through any hearts that are touched by this message!

I am grateful to our Blessed Mother for her example. I am confident that she has molded me as her daughter and carried me to her Son. I pray she will continue to do so more intimately.

Most gracious thanks to my earthly mother. She planted the seeds of faith within me from the beginning of life. Her healing and strength in recent years has been nothing less than inspiring. I am blessed to walk the road to Christ alongside her as she offers me continued strength for the journey. She is one of my best friends and I am so proud of her.

Thank you to all of the friends and family who have been so supportive in this process of writing Woman In Love. Thank you especially to those of you who read this manuscript and offered your thoughts and prayers. Special thanks to Caroline Bernard, Steve Bollman, Shelley Garza, Rhonda Gruenewald, Stephanie Hartfiel, Donny Holender, Alexandra Jung, Olivia Jung, Melinda Lynch, Brendan Lynch, Jim Mahoney, Barb Mahoney, Eric Mueller, and Father Victor Perez.

Of course, thank you to my husband Mark, for your contributions to this book. But most of all, thank you for saving me from myself. You continue to challenge me to holiness every day. Thank you for teaching our daughters to be Women In Love. I could not have asked for a greater gift to give to my children. I love you!

Table Of Contents

Woman In Love

Forward

One of the benefits of working in ministry is the opportunity to meet some truly wonderful individuals. Two such individuals are Mark and Katie Hartfiel.

I met Mark and Katie in early 2005. They had just gotten married after graduating from Franciscan University in Steubenville, Ohio. Katie accepted a job as a youth minister at Saint Cecilia Catholic Church in Houston, Texas and after a short stint at an accounting firm, Mark came to work with me coordinating the That Man is You! men's ministry. Katie helped to develop the youth program at Saint Cecilia's into one of the most dynamic in the country with hundreds of teenagers gathering weekly. Mark has assisted in the growth of the That Man is You! program into a truly national ministry. Quite simply, it would not exist as it does today were it not for the work of Mark Hartfiel. As such, I am fond of saying, "If the world had a few more Mark and Katie Hartfiels, it would be a better place." Indeed, Mark and Katie are already busy making it a better place.

Although Mark and Katie made an immediate impact on their respective ministries, only over time did I come to understand their journey in becoming the wonderful couple that they are today.

Forward • Woman In Love

It is a story so compelling it deserves to be told far and wide. It is the story about the dreams of a young girl and the love and hope that sustained those dreams through struggle and hardship.

When Katie's father decided to divorce her mother, their family life was turned upside down. The reality of their new life was not pretty. Indeed, it was enough to snuff out dreams, to even shrink the human heart so it doesn't dare to dream. This new reality could have turned this young girl into another statistic: broken home, troubled youth, unwanted pregnancy, illegitimate child or a broken home in the next generation.

Fortunately, Katie forgot to read the storyline. Her life travels a different path. She anchors her hope in a merciful God who loves her. She trusts that God will fulfill her dreams, the dreams of a future husband and the family life they will share together.

Perhaps what is most amazing about Katie's story is that God used Katie's faith and trust to transform an everyday man into the man of her dreams. Through faith, God transformed Katie into the woman worthy of the man of her dreams. The Lord lays the foundation for the family life she dreamt to have with her Husband-To-Be.

As such, Katie's story becomes a light shining in the darkness for our modern culture. To a whole new generation, Katie's story says, "Don't allow pain and sorrow and disappointment to have the last word. Don't allow your dreams to die. Don't allow your heart to shrink. Trust in God. Dreams can come true. He is that good."

I suspect a whole new generation of young women will "get it" and begin keeping a journal to their "Husband-To-Be." I suspect that in the process these girls will be fashioned into women worthy of the men of their dreams. Furthermore, I suspect that countless young men will suddenly experience the grace to be transformed.

When all of this happens, the world will become a better place.

Thank you Mark and Katie.

Steve Bollman
Founder and President, Paradisus Dei
Developer, That Man is You!

Chapter 1

My First Love

"Purity prepares the soul for love and love confirms the soul in purity."

— *St. John Henry Cardinal Newman*

Chapter 1 • Woman In Love

12-27-04

Dear HTB,

My Future Husband,

My Best Friend,

My Rock,

Wow, I can't believe I am writing my last letter. I have been waiting a long time for this moment, and here it is. If you are reading this it means that tomorrow we will be man and wife! You may be wondering what all of this means... As I've told you before, during my junior year of high school, I began praying for my HTB (Husband-To-Be) on a regular basis. What I didn't tell you was that I also began writing you letters. So many times I needed you and missed you so desperately that I would try and satisfy my longing by some sort of communication with you. I turned to this notebook. My goal was to form my understanding of my husband into a concrete individual who was really living in time and space. That person turned out to be you, Mark Hartfiel, who was meanwhile existing in the Lone Star state.

Many of the letters in the first half of my journal to you are a little depressing. They are full of plenty of whining and venting to the man I was yet to meet. I considered removing some of them but I didn't really think that was very fair. I give you all of my past, present and future, and that is what this is all about. You will meet me as a 17 year old (and barely 17 at that!) and watch me grow into Mrs. Mark Hartfiel. I've been yours for longer than you could possibly imagine.

Throughout all these years and all these pages, I could never have imagined a recipient such as you. You are such proof to me that God's generosity can always and will always exceed our expectations. Mark, I wish I could express how elated I am that it is you.

I love you with all that I am, and that is what I give to you. I've loved and respected you since before you had a face. You are my gift. You are my reason. You are my everything and I want to share it all with you.

You have helped me understand Mary's role in my life in that being closer to you means being closer to Jesus. You make me want to be holy. As we give each other everything tomorrow, let's give each other the promise of Heaven as well.

Know that I am praying for you. I have waited and I am so glad that I don't have to wait anymore.

I love you,

Me

Chapter 1 • Woman In Love

Welcome to the revolution. This isn't just another purity book. In the pages that follow, you will find a new approach to sexual purity. Yes, we will discuss the temptations against chastity and some ways to tackle them. More importantly, we will establish a motivation for abstinence that will change your outlook forever. As you read the following pages, you can rest assured that I am praying for you and for your future spouse.

That's right, your future spouse. One day, he will be everything to you, and your world will never return to what it was before he knew you. He will have one mission in life and that is to deliver you to Heaven. Everything else within his life will fall under that premise, and you will be the queen of his heart. Right now, at this very moment, somewhere in the world, he has a name.

Yes, your vocation has a name. This name was spoken when the Lord breathed you into being within your mother's womb. Your Creator set out a perfect plan for your life ending with a triumphant "happily ever after" as you fall back into the Father's arms at your death.

"For I know well the plans I have in mind for you, says the Lord, plans for your welfare, not for woe! Plans to give you a future full of hope" (Jer. 29:11).[1] Your Creator knows the ins and the outs of every strength, limitation, need and longing. He put them there. Wouldn't it make sense that the Lord who knows you perfectly could fashion a partner that was best for you? God knit you together in your mother's womb (Ps 139:3). At that moment He knew the name of the vocation which would carry you safely back to Him.

When I was seventeen years old, this truth became very real to me. I felt that if God knew me so well, then surely He knew the best way for me to return to Him. Certainly, within His omnipotent knowledge, God knew that I would marry and who I would marry. If this were true, then that boy must be out there somewhere! I started to ask myself:

> *"What is he doing at this very moment?*
> *Where does he live?*
> *What is he passionate about?*
> *Did he think about me today?*
> *What is he struggling with?"*

I figured he was probably close to my age and facing the same difficulties that I witnessed and experienced every day. Knowing how hard it was to live in the midst of this culture, I concluded that it must be difficult for him, as well. If all of this were true surely he needed my prayers.

Does this mean there is only one person for you? Maybe... then again maybe not. What it does mean is that the Lord knows everything. He stands outside of time and is intimately aware of every breath you will take. He knows the decisions you will make. He knows the man you will marry, and He knows where your Husband-To-Be is at this very moment. He would love to shower grace upon him in response to your prayers.

KATIE'S STORY

My conviction began when I was selected to participate in a leadership and discipleship training week in Denver with a few of my friends. I joined 35 other teens from around the country for incredible spiritual formation, the Sacraments, and amazing fellowship. We prayed, sang, laughed and ate, and then we prayed and sang some more. Some of the most memorable parts of the week were in the silent moments I spent with my journal in front of the Blessed Sacrament. It was here that I looked at the face that I wanted to gaze at forever. He consumed me more profoundly than I had ever consumed Him. I fell in love that week. This love had a face and a name. He was a person I could pour myself into while

Chapter 1 • Woman In Love

He filled me until I was overflowing. I couldn't get enough. The elation that He brought me was more indescribable than anything I had ever experienced. This Love came with a capital L. The Lord, Love Himself, was revealed to me, and there was no turning back. I came home feeling alive for the first time and all I knew was that I wanted more.

Only five boys were part of the group, and their love for the Lord was extremely inspiring. It opened my heart even more to the yearning for a man that would love Christ more than he could ever love me. The pages of my journal began to encompass more and more prayers, asking that the man who would capture my heart would first be captured by His. It was during this week that I made my final resolve. My mission was to be a warrior for my future husband. I would arm him in prayer to the best of my ability.

So I hit my knees. Each night I would beg God for specific intentions for my Husband-To-Be (or as I began to refer to him, my HTB). If he was struggling with poor decisions, friendships, bad influences, or impurity, I pleaded with God to grant grace for conversion. I asked that God would reveal Himself to him, as I had been so blessed to experience Christ in my own life.

When I discovered this, I decided that if my future spouse was out there, I didn't want to waste my heart on anyone else. I was not foolish enough to think that I wouldn't have to kiss some frogs to find my prince. However, I did know that I had an end goal in mind and I didn't want to be distracted. So, I began to write. I wanted my HTB to be tangible in some way. I wanted to better understand him as a concrete reality, and not a lofty romantic idea. It was then that I started to put the longings of my heart on paper. I found myself falling in love with a young man who was unbeknownst to me. What started as some loose leaf musings turned into a prized possession. In his absence I expressed my loneliness, brokenness and struggles, along with the joys of my heart. I explained who I wanted to be for him and what I wanted to share.

I told him the ways the Lord was working in my life and how He was challenging me to trust. The pages began to fill with my joys, my vulnerabilities, my fears, my hopes, my dreams, and ultimately my prayers.

Meanwhile, a senior teenage boy in a Houston suburb was unknowingly receiving grace from prayers being uttered over a thousand miles away...

MARK'S STORY

My life throughout high school consisted of a few things: basketball, friends, parties, girls and beer. Not to over exaggerate, I wasn't completely wretched, but I was just the typical "cool" kid. Popularity in high school came quite naturally to me, and I seemed to enjoy and take advantage of it. My biggest dilemma and concern in those days was where the party was that weekend. I vividly remember walking through the halls on a Monday and already talking to friends about what we were going to do for the weekend. Looking back, I don't think I really thought much about anything besides having fun and partaking in any activity that made me feel good. I will spare you from reading all the details of my personal sins, but I will define my attitude and lifestyle in one word... *pleasure*. If it feels good, do it. That is what my entire group of friends and I lived by. It is not unlike how much of the world still lives today. I was a person who had experienced the pleasures of the world, was accepted and liked by the world, and thought I had everything I needed. I certainly was not thinking about my wife-to-be or trying to prepare for my gift of self to her one day.

One miraculous summer night, my life changed through an incredible encounter. It was the summer before my freshman year of college, and I was on my way to play college basketball. This was the time I had dreamed of since my dad first put the ball in my hands at the age of three. It was a typical summer. I was rolling along, playing ball, working out, and having fun. Out of nowhere, one night, while I was taking a shower, something happened that I will never forget. I wasn't in prayer. Nothing was out of the ordinary about this night, but what happened next changed my life forever.

In an instant, I felt the Holy Spirit rush into the room and into my heart. It was as if I was completely blind before and now I could see. The scales of blindness were removed from my eyes, and I could see with more clarity than any moment before. I experienced extreme sorrow and contrition, mixed with a supernatural joy. My sins rushed through my head and heart, while simultaneously I was given the grace to know God was merciful. In that moment, I understood with clarity a simple reality: Jesus Christ died personally for my sins. I had heard this statement many times before, but my heart had never been truly pierced by this reality. My God was personal. He had a name and a face. He lived, laughed, wept, and ultimately died on a cross...*all for me*. The clarity and grace I experienced that night was enough for me to change my life immediately and with urgency. I instantly fell to my knees for an amount of time of which I am still unsure. Before I left the shower that night, I realized Jesus Christ was worthy of my life and I promised Him I would change. I was struck with a sudden call to conversion, which seemed to have no natural explanation. I experienced a deep and consuming love that could have only been an authentic encounter with the Living God. I knew without a doubt that someone, somewhere was praying for me in a major way.

YOUR STORY

This book is about the journey. It is meant to be a guide as you walk in these vital days of preparation for your vocation. At this very moment, the Lord is fashioning you as a potter pours himself into a masterpiece. You aren't waiting for life to begin; your love story starts now!

The two stories in the last few pages are so different. Your story is just as unique. I don't know where you are coming from, but wherever you have been, the Lord's mercy wants to envelop and overwhelm you.

At the end of each chapter of this book, you will be given a spiritual application followed by an opportunity to write. This section will be titled "Dear HTB". This is a chance for you to be molded by your First Love, the Lord, and prepared for your Second Love, your future spouse. Grab a journal, a spiral or a three ring notebook, and partner with the Lord as you write your love story together.

The most important thing that you can do for your spouse is pray for him. Crawl into the trenches of the spiritual battle raging over his soul and be a warrior for him, which means being courageous. The day has arrived for you to stand up for your Husband-To-Be and pray for him with vigor. As you arm yourself to fight for him, remember what author Ambrose Redmoon says, "Courage is not the absence of fear, but rather the judgment that something else is more important than fear."

So what confidence can you take with you as we go forward from here? The answer is simple: Christ has already won the battle, and His victory is ours for the taking. Take Christ as your First Love and trust Him with your total gift of self today.

Find a quiet place and open your journal and your heart. Begin in prayer, begging the Lord to provide for your future spouse and to do so in the way that He sees fit. Tell the Lord that you trust His plans and His timing. Tell the Lord that you want to say "yes" to Him when He calls. Now, begin to write the letters that your Husband-To-Be will read the night before you give yourself to him in marriage. Tell him that you are praying Jeremiah 29:11 for him today: "For I know well the plans I have in mind for you, says the Lord, plans for your welfare, not for woe! Plans to give you a future full of hope." Tell him what that means to you and how you hope that you will fit into that plan.

Tell your HTB you love him even now and that you are honored to wait for him...

Woman In Love

Chapter 2

God's Faithfulness in Suffering

"He said to me, 'My grace is sufficient for you, for power is made perfect in weakness.' I will rather boast most gladly of my weaknesses, in order that the power of Christ may dwell with me."

-2 Corinthians 12:9

Chapter 2 • Woman In Love

My senior year started out perfectly. I had an incredible community at my parish, a great schedule at school, uplifting friendships, and a 1988 Mercury Sable that was as ugly as sin. It only started about three-quarters of the time but took my friends and me wherever our teenage hearts desired. My family was always very active at church. My brother and I volunteered for Sunday school and then sang in the youth choir at Mass. My dad was an usher, and my mom was an active volunteer. The school year rolled into the fall months when I started to notice a sudden change in my mother's demeanor. She wasn't present to the world, and it always seemed that she was elsewhere mentally. One afternoon, I found her sitting in the backyard staring into nothingness. I asked her what was bothering her, and her answer changed my life forever. My father had left her a note. He told her that he didn't love her anymore and that he wanted to leave. She swore me to secrecy. No one could know that I was aware of this situation: not my friends, not my extended family, and not even my father.

Then, a funny thing happened. He didn't leave. He left the note and made his intentions known, yet packed no bags and made no move. I would go to school and church and spend time with my family and friends, all the while pretending as if the world was not falling apart around me. In the meantime, I became my mother's confidant. She would tell me things about their relationship past and present that no child should bear. This went on for months until I woke up on a school morning to a shrieking fight between my parents. My younger brother and I came into the kitchen to find an ugly scene as the truth was hurled into our faces. We were crudely informed that our father had begun a new life with a new woman whom he preferred to his life with us. My father stood silent and then began to justify his actions by describing his misery in our home. He explained that if we loved him, we would want his happiness. My mother responded that he may as well have left us to die. Hearing that, I grabbed my backpack and headed to my car so that I wouldn't be late for school. Days began and ended, plagued with nausea, as I smiled at my friends and classmates and pretended that everything was fine.

January came and the pressure was amplified. I constantly broke out in hives from the duplicity and stress. My dad moved to a cabin in the mountains and explained that he was heading there to pray and listen to the Lord. I was finally allowed to tell a few close friends, as long as they agreed to keep the story to themselves. My dad would come home and pretend that he lived at our house for key social events such as my 18th birthday party and finally my high school graduation. We would all smile and play along.

I decided to live at home for my freshmen year and attend the local university. The agony continued throughout the year as the situation seemed to worsen. We discovered that my dad was living in the mountains, not only with the rosaries and devotionals we had sent with him, but with the woman he had sworn was out of his life. He eventually moved back to town, and the secret was revealed.

My poor dispirited mother spiraled down a path that could have led to mental destruction. She would hide in her room for days at a time. In her mental absence, I made sure that she and my brother were fed. I brought meals home from my part-time waitressing job and gave my brother his lunch money. I helped my brother with his homework and gave him rides to school and social events. He and I would sit on my bed late into the night and talk about our pains and resolve to fight our way through it together.

Finally, the summer after my freshmen year of college, the divorce hit the courts. Possessions were split and financially things became very tight for us. The most difficult part of the court process, on a personal level, was the fact that my father chose to remain monetarily responsible for my younger brother and legally emancipate me. This process lifted all responsibility toward me as his child. It felt like a reverse adoption. My dad was releasing himself from a legal connection to me, and it seemed he was abandoning me all over again.

Often times, I would turn to the person I knew I could trust, though he didn't respond at the time. The pages of my notebook to my Husband-To-Be were often a substitute for his comforting arms. At the time, my sense of security in the present was tested, but my hope for my future was secure. I expressed my feelings and fears on sheet after sheet of college rule, as I begged the Lord to spare me this pain in my own future family years later.

In turning to my HTB, I attempted to abandon myself to the Lord. I knew that He had blessed me in an excessive way in the years that preceded this horrendous time in my life. I could see that He had prepared my heart for the brokenness that was to come. He had built my spiritual muscles to withstand such trials, and for that, I was incredibly grateful. I knew that I had done nothing to deserve this preemptive grace, but I couldn't thank the Lord enough for giving it to me. Incredible people had been placed in my path that helped form my prayer life and relationship with the Lord. When the hurricane winds came, a strong foundation held me together.

So in response to the storm that raged around me, I would turn to the Lord in prayer. I begged and begged Him to turn things around. I tore my heart out in desperation as I pleaded each night for the conversion of my father's heart. I began asking the Saints to join me in this mission as I would pray nine-day novenas asking for an out-pouring of grace. The days would draw to a close and I would begin another crusade imploring a different Saint to come to his aid. Months passed, and rather than a change of heart, things continued to worsen. Eventually, I couldn't handle the apparent rejection any longer. I told the Lord that I was happy to be diligent in my prayer time with Him. I would joyfully continue my commitments to the parish that I loved so dearly. I would praise Him, honor Him and love Him, but I would no longer ask Him for His help for my father.

Weeks turned into months, as I withheld my intentions from the Lord. I will never forget a particular night that I spent in prayer. I had a stubborn intention to hold back my prayers for my dad. A thought came to me with such clarity and conviction that I have never doubted it came from the Lord. I knew in that moment that He had heard every agonizing prayer that poured from my heart. In fact, He was crying with me. He was hiding me within His redeeming wounds. He assured me that He hadn't just given my dad the grace that I had asked for; rather, He overwhelmed him with a superabundance of it. That night in prayer I felt as though the Lord was showing me that my father was holding an umbrella over his head in order to avoid contact with the grace and the mercy of the Lord. I learned two things through this revelation. The first was a realization that I couldn't cease in prayer for my dad. If at any moment there was an opening of vulnerability and that umbrella came down for an instant, the mercy needed to be there to consume him. The other was that I needed to start looking for the areas in my own life where I was rejecting God's gift of Divine Life within me.

These two lessons became integral in my search for my vocation. There was another man for whom I was holding on to hope. As my image and example of husband and father was ripped to shreds, my hopes for the future also became cloudy. My motivation in prayer for my HTB became more important than ever. I needed the Lord to shower that same superabundance of grace and mercy on the man He was preparing for me, wherever he may be.

YOUR STORY

I've prayed and discerned so much in the decision to share my story. You may or may not be able to relate to the experiences you have read here. Perhaps your struggles differ in some way. You may be someone who has experienced death in your family or struggled with depression or loneliness. It is possible that an illness has struck you or a family member, and it has brought about great pains in your life. Whether it be relationships, guilt, fear, pressures, stress, or even just an unexplainable emptiness in your life, I have one thing to offer to you in the pages that follow… **hope**. Any personal reflection on my own experiences and my own failings can only lead me to one place, and that is a recognition that it is "in my weakness, He is strong" (2 Cor. 12:10). The bottom-line of this statement is that the Lord is faithful. He knows the plans He has for you. The Lord doesn't ***make*** bad things happen in our lives, but He can ***always*** use them for a greater good if we let Him. All we have to do is let down our umbrellas and give him that chance.

"Always be ready to give an explanation to anyone who asks you for a reason for your hope, but do it with gentleness and reverence."
- 1 Peter 3:15-16

A faith story is commonly called a "testimony." If you are reading this book, it is most likely because you have encountered the Lord on some level. Perhaps it is a new and developing flame or a raging fire that has been fueled for some time. Possibly your relationship with the Lord has burned brightly in the past, but has grown lukewarm. What is your story?

Saint Peter tells us that we should be ever ready to share our testimony so that we can give witness to the hope that we have. This may require some general reflection and prayer in order to develop a concise and structured account. If someone were to ask you why you believed in the promises of Christ, would you have an answer?

Share your reason for hope with your HTB today. Before you begin to write, take some time in prayer and contemplation. Why do you desire to follow the Lord? How has He touched your heart? When have you encountered Him? What was life like before He entered your life in a personal way? How has it been different since? They say you can't have a testimony without a test. What struggles kept you from the Lord before your "conversion," and what temptations have plagued you since?

Don't worry if you haven't had an earth-shattering experience in your faith. Remember, God gives us what we need when we need it. Jesus even says, "Blessed are they who have not seen yet have believed" (John 20:29). If this applies to you, do not fail to thank God for the gift of faith He has given you!

Chapter 2 • Woman In Love

Relay your story to your HTB, but don't stop there. The beautiful thing about Christianity is that we remain unfinished until we arrive in Heaven. You are living in the middle of your testimony! Tell your HTB what the Lord is doing in your life right now. I've heard it said that the moment you realize that you are comfortable in your faith is the moment you should try to move forward. How is God calling you to deepen your faith right now?

Explain the ways that you hope your HTB will fit into your testimony. How do you hope he will lead you to holiness? In what ways do you hope he will challenge you to grow?

End with an assertion that you will be praying for your HTB as God fashions his personal testimony as well.

Tell your HTB you love him even now and that you are honored to wait for him...

Woman
In
Love

Chapter 3

On My Own and All Alone

"...I will never forsake you or abandon you."

-Hebrews 13:5

Chapter 3 • Woman In Love

My parent's marriage and the summer came to a close within a few months of one another. The whirlpool that had been pulling me inward and downward was about to release its grip, as I prepared to transfer to another school and leave home. Some kids dream of becoming an astronaut, attending an Ivy League school, or traveling the world. From the time I was 16 years old, I had set my sights on Franciscan University in Steubenville, Ohio. I felt that the Lord shared in my desire, and it was finally my chance to answer His call. I packed up and headed for the Midwest, hoping to find healing and freedom.

I'll never forget the intense anticipation that animated me as we drove up the curvy road to my new home. Right from the beginning, Franciscan proved to be exactly what I had hoped. I met incredible people who were striving for holiness. I loved my classes and reveled in the good conversation and stimulating relationships all around me. From eating salsa and Wheat Thins from a mini-fridge at three a.m. to the unending study sessions, I savored the college lifestyle.

Near the beginning of the school year, I wrote to my future husband:

"I can't help but wonder if you are nearby. I wonder if I know you, if I've passed you without even knowing it is you with whom I was exchanging smiles. You might be in a building nearby right now or even living in a building in which I have walked."

Boxes were unpacked, spilling their contents into an over-stuffed 10 ft x 14 ft room. Simultaneously, this new atmosphere challenged me to open myself and unveil that which was within me. As my time away from the toxicity in Colorado grew, my woundedness became more and more apparent. Like adding an elegant piece of furniture to a dingy living room, these bright new aspects in life cast attention on the darker parts remaining. Brick by brick a fortress had been constructed to surround my heart in order to survive the preceding two years. I quickly discovered that this armor was so impenetrable even I couldn't figure out how to disarm it. Jaded by my past, I knew I was unable to endure any further pain or rejection.

One evening, I found myself in prayer begging for freedom. Like the Israelites imprisoned in Old Testament Egypt, I longed to hear the trumpet declaring that my time of slavery had ended. Suddenly, the Lord gave me a moment of clarity: this freedom was already mine! In my mind's eye, I developed an image of myself imprisoned in a cage separating me from the life I desired. Oddly enough, I discovered that the door of the cage was open. Nothing prevented my departure, except my crippling fear. Paralyzed by the trepidation of what lay beyond, I was surprised at my response. Rather than dashing for the door, I found myself shrinking to the furthest corner of my cell. I wasn't capable of venturing out into a world where I would allow my heart to become wounded once again.

They say that college is one of the most formative periods of your life, second only to your first few years after birth. I was ready to find out what that would mean on a personal level and to discover who would share it with me. The beginning of the university school year is a breeding ground for new friendships. Everyone is ready to socialize and make as many new acquaintances as possible to fill the social void lurking in each newly transplanted student's life.

I found that I was meeting tons of people in the first few weeks of school, but I was having a hard time developing real friendships. It was time to try a new strategy outside of the organized social minglings happening daily around campus. I decided that in each class I would try to strike up a conversation with the people seated around me in an attempt to form some solid relationships. In one class in particular, I found my seat-mates seemingly uninterested in being my friend, or at least uninterested in my small talk. It was my first Theology class on campus and I had actually squeezed it into my schedule just a few days before classes had begun. I decided that the next time I came into the room I would pick a new seat in order to acquire a new group of potential friends fresh for the picking. I quickly scanned the class and found my golden opportunity, a seat next to a good looking guy toward the center of the room.

The seat change proved to be genius. I was soon making chitchat with my new crop of classmates in Principles of Biblical Studies 201…all except for the tall, dark, handsome type seated right next to me. I found that I was too nervous to venture into conversation with him and hoped I would eventually find some courage. What happened instead was much more uncomfortable than a simple hello during class. I started seeing my new-seat-neighbor everywhere on campus. The awkwardness grew during each encounter, as we both seemed to be aware that we recognized one another but had never spoken. I had an internal battle at each passing. Do I smile? Say Hello? Throw a head nod? Avoid eye contact? The result tended to be a graceless combination of all of the above in one distressing gesture of weirdness.

Shortly afterwards, I decided it was time to take action. This would be the day that I would muster all my confidence and introduce myself. The class period ended, and before I had a chance to gather my books and my nerves my mysterious friend was out the door. I began my internal pep talk, explaining to myself that the *next* class period would surely be my chance. I walked out the door to find the 6'2" unidentified student waiting outside for me in the hall. He smiled and explained that he'd seen me everywhere and thought it was time to make an introduction. I clumsily agreed, as we began walking together in the direction of the cafeteria. It turned out that Mark Hartfiel and I had eerily similar daily schedules. We had classes around the same time in the same buildings, tended to eat lunch simultaneously and even attended daily Mass at the same time each day.

Thus the routine was born. We would meet up in class, walk to the cafeteria and sit together at lunch. We would then pray or study together during our free period that followed and finish with Mass before afternoon classes. Our Principles of Biblical Studies class proved to be a bit challenging for me, and I was lucky to have a study-buddy for whom the material came naturally. It wasn't long before all of these factors budded into a solid and comforting friendship.

Not much time passed before it became evident that our compatibility seemed to make sense on more than a platonic level. Mark and I enjoyed our time together, and it was no secret to one another or to our friends. We laughed together yet shared so much depth in our conversations that would often drift long into the evening. Something was happening in both of our hearts. For Mark, it was exciting and electrifying. For me, it was terrifying. All of the emotions from the last two years exploded within me, taunting me with doubts about the reality of a love that could bear all things, believe all things, and endure all things.

YOUR STORY

Much of this book will be centered on the virtue of chastity. Pope John Paul II defines chastity as the recognition that our sexual desires are always subordinate to the true love and dignity of another person. He goes on to tell us, "Chastity is a difficult long-term matter; one must wait patiently for it to bear fruit for the happiness of loving kindness which it must bring. But at the same time chastity is the sure way to happiness."

There is no doubt that my single years were lonely. Yes, I was convicted that the Lord knew who I would marry and that this man was out there. Often times this thought was comforting, other times it seemed to make the time of waiting more difficult. Patience was a gift that I would ask for regularly.

Chapter 3 • Woman In Love

The pursuit and discernment of our vocation is a process. The process molds us. The Holy Father affirms that chastity itself is a "difficult and long term matter". It is easy to look back and thank God for the journey once the Lord has delivered His answer. However, the time leading up to the revelation of God's Will can sometimes be seemingly torturous.

It is important to embrace and recognize the difficulty, but simultaneously hold on to the promise. Regardless of the vocation that you have been molded for, the Lord is calling you to chastity. Just as Pope John Paul II explained, "…chastity is the sure way to happiness." Never forget to search for the joy that the virtue of chastity has to offer, especially when loneliness comes knocking.

Dear HTB,

Express your desire for your future spouse as you write today. Take time to dwell on your feelings and don't stifle them. If you are lonely, say so. If you miss him, tell him. Distance makes the heart grow fonder. Allow these emotions to increase your dedication to your mission of chastity. Let your heart long for the romance that is still to come. Don't stop there. Reflect on the happiness of the present and the happiness in the future. Express your willingness to hold out for the best, no matter what the cost.

Tell your HTB you love him even now and that you are honored to wait for him...

Woman In Love

Chapter 4

Wounded and In Love

"The Lord is close to the brokenhearted, saves those whose spirit it crushed."

—Psalm 34:19

Chapter 4 • Woman In Love

The fall began to take hold of the state of Ohio, and the trees on every foggy hill of the valley seemed to be on fire with color. The weather was brisk and perfect. The students were content to stroll to class in sweaters and scarves as their winter coats anxiously awaited their turn on the racks of the dormitory closets. Parent's Weekend arrived, and the campus was alive with activities and excitement. Families were reunited for the first time since bidding farewell in August. I prepared for a lonely weekend, as everyone planned to show their guests around campus and participate in the events. I decided to attend the large and vibrant Friday night Mass by myself that evening. I felt strange as I walked alone toward the large field house where sizeable crowds could gather for worship.

As Mass concluded, I attempted to navigate my way through the crowds back to my empty dorm room. As I was exiting the field house, I surprisingly made eye contact with a familiar face. My glance was met with a friendly Texan smile. My aisle converged with Mark's at the perfect moment and in this crowd I was introduced to his parents for the first time. He had described them perfectly, and their kindness was evident as we left the building together. Mark explained that he had invited a number of people to join his parents for dinner and asked if I wanted to come along. Relieved that I had evaded an evening of quality time with my laptop, I agreed without hesitation.

We arrived only to discover that every other guest of Mark's had somehow made other plans. Suddenly I was alone with this 21 year-old handsome bachelor and his parents. Choices were slim as Steubenville had few restaurants, and those were packed to the brim with visitors. The situation grew more interesting as we found a table in a dim-lit, smoke-filled sports bar. I was intrigued to observe Mark's interaction with his parents. They discussed siblings, school, and their cattle ranches in Texas. The conversation drifted toward his mother's preparations for her Masters Degree in Pastoral Studies. She described some recent studies on marriage and family, and all became engaged in their personal ideas and reflections. Mark stated he had recently heard a deacon explain that when he asked engaged couples why they wanted to be married the answer was always the same, "She makes me so happy" or "He makes me so happy." With a twisted face, Mark went on to explain, "When I get married it won't be like that. My response will be that I want to make *her* so happy." I am not sure if my face reflected my disbelief, but I certainly hoped it didn't. Who was this man sitting beside me? I was amazed!

The evening ended, and Mark's parents dropped us off on campus. I expected Mark to bid me farewell and carry on with his weekend. Instead, we started walking and talking until Friday turned into Saturday. In hindsight, it was clear that this weekend was a turning point in our friendship, as we began to journey together on a different road toward our future. Years later, in his toast at our rehearsal dinner, Mark's dad would explain their reaction when they left us in the rearview mirror and drove up and down the hills of the Ohio River Valley. He said he knew with utter certainty that something epic was happening between his youngest son and this girl from Colorado.

As time passed, Mark became my very best friend on campus. I began to open up to him and discovered a true sense of authenticity and freedom living within him. All of our interactions were completely platonic. Mark respected me deeply, and he showed me with his words and actions. Our friendship deepened on a spiritual level which spilled over into every aspect of our relationship.

The months that followed were both beautiful and excruciating. In my letters to my HTB I wrote about my fears and baggage. I knew that I didn't want him to bear the burden with me. My suffering had been too great. I wanted to offer my whole heart to my Husband-To-Be, not the broken sloppy mess that currently lay within my chest. I didn't want him to have to share in the suffering, only the victory. The problem was that I had been utterly unsuccessful in achieving that victory on my own. In my letters to

Chapter 4 • Woman In Love

my HTB I wrote,

"...this book is filled with pages of lack of trust and patience as I wait for you. I have come to a new conclusion: I don't want you yet. I don't want anyone yet. I am an absolute mess. I have nothing to give and I do not know how to receive. God has so much work to do if I will only let Him!

...I want to give you so much. I want to make you happy, and I want to serve you. I can do none of this right now; I am willing to accept that...I love you, and I am so excited to meet you. So, right now I am going to try to make myself into a woman of God, first for Him and then for you. I'm waiting, and I am trying to grow during this time of struggle because it is a gift, and one that will not last forever! I can only hope that I will use this time sufficiently to prepare myself for you."

My relationship with Mark was revitalizing and gave me the desire to approach the door of that cage. But desire wasn't enough and rather than run for freedom, I became a recluse in the further corners of darkness. Following every positive experience pointing toward a romantic connection, I would tend to overcorrect to avoid sending the wrong message about my emotional availability. I was falling in love with Mark, yet the only thing keeping him from me was me. It was the first time in my life that I was closed off to relationship. For years I had been longing for romantic companionship and spiritual friendship on an intimate level, and now the perfect candidate stood before me. However, I was in no position to reciprocate. I simply couldn't bring myself to allow anyone into my heart if it would mean the opportunity to rip it out and take it with him down the road.

I wasn't the only one musing in a journal during this pivotal semester. In Mark's prayers in December of that year he wrote to the Lord,

"I give you all of my relationships Lord and beg for your Will. I especially put in your hands my relationship with Katie. But more importantly I beg that you heal her and give her freedom. Cut down the lies that she believes and the lack of trust. Heal her from her past family situations and make her new."

The semester started to come to a close. In my last letter of 2002, I let my broken heart do the talking.

"I can't help but wonder what all of this will do to our future family. How will my pain affect our children? Right now I am dependent only on myself because I have been left alone. From this point forward, I can't rely on anyone but myself because I can't abandon myself like everyone else has. Even my family has left me, and if that is true how can I ever trust you not to do the same? I want to. I want to but this would make me vulnerable. I don't know that I can do that again.

By the time you read this I want to be healed. Not for myself but so that I can give myself to you. I want to be flesh of your flesh and one body with you, and when I think about that right now, all I see is my own inability. I don't want to bring all of this into a relationship with you. When we become one, I don't want this struggle to be a part of you. I wouldn't want it for anyone.

If there is something I have learned over these last few years it is that life is not easy. I know life with you will be wonderful, but it will not be perfect. I have so many flaws; I apologize already for anything that I may do to hurt you, but please love me forever...Love the Christ in me.

I love you already and I know the day will come when I can serve and complement you. I know it will come at the perfect time. I look forward to being yours and I pray for you daily.

I love and miss you and may God bless you my love. I am waiting for you!"

Chapter 4 • Woman In Love

Just a few short weeks after penning this letter, Mark reached a breaking point. I had driven him to a state of utter confusion and doubt. He wanted clarity, and rightfully so. It was the eve of Christmas break, and a long month stretched ahead of us in our far-off hometowns. What unfolded was the painful reality of the bloody battleground that was my heart. In his charming southern drawl, he divulged his intentions for the future and the man he desired to be for me. My reply to each assertion was a bitter rejection to the possibility of anyone feeling the way he did about me. I told him I couldn't let him into my heart and that he shouldn't wait for me. In a moment of desperation for his understanding I explained that I'd heard the phrase "It's better to have loved and lost than to never have loved at all." I told him I would rather die alone than to have loved someone and lost them.

In that moment, Mark realized the truth. He saw the magnitude of my pain. I would assume that most people would therefore declare with conviction, "This girl has issues," and run for the hills. It was one of the million times I would come to see that Mark wasn't "most people". He explained to me later that in this moment his entire mission surrounding his intentions for me changed. Mark let go of his own desires and focused himself completely on my brokenness. He took up his yoke and the burden it was connected to and began to walk this road with me. He ached to offer himself for my healing regardless of the pain and price that he would have to pay. He relayed this to the Lord as he wrote:

"Lord, I continue to ask for your blessings upon Katie's family and their situation. It breaks my heart to see people going through rough times. Lord, guide them with your Spirit and bring them peace. I will do whatever I need to do to help her. Heal her, Lord, from all her wounds and allow her to trust in the beauty of families."

Recognizing the incredible man that sat beside me on a cold bench that December night, I must admit that a heavy guilt laid in my chest. I watched his heart break by my own hand. I knew full well that he bore no fault as the ripple of the events of my family shattered someone who had never even met them. In an attempt to offer comfort, I explained that this reality was all about me. The cliché line, "It isn't you, it's me" encompassed my message. His response was surprising but true. "It *is* me. You say that, but I am the one that you won't trust, I am the one that you won't let into your heart. You say that it is you, but you can't stay isolated when someone cares as much about you as I do. It *is* about me."

I later understood that this was the same message the Lord was speaking to me as well. My hardened heart was breaking His heart of mercy. My rejection and fear of healing and freedom was causing Christ great pain. In an attempt to internalize the burden, I placed the load on my own shoulders. I had forgotten that the only way to redemption was to watch that brokenness be lifted and placed on the one who could take it to Calvary. In that same moment, the Lord, my First Love, was saying, "Katie, it *is* me. I am the one that you won't trust. I am the one that you won't let into your heart. You say that it is you, but you can't stay isolated when someone cares as much about you as I do. It *is* about me."

I had spent so much time and energy imposing my own ideas upon the Will of God. I had decided that I wanted to be clean and whole before I entered into a relationship. It was my own pride and selfishness that was failing to recognize the path of healing that was laid before me. Thankfully, both Christ and Mark were not about to give up on me yet. My Father in Heaven would soon use this man, His handiwork, to bring about a new life in me.

YOUR STORY

"Trust in the Lord with all your heart, on your own intelligence rely not. In all your ways be mindful of Him, and He will make straight your paths." -Proverbs 3:5

Chapter 4 • Woman In Love

When you pray about your vocation, are you afraid of the answer the Lord will give? Has He ever shown Himself to be untrustworthy? If you give Him the chance, the Lord will guide you to the vocation that will bring you the most joy in your life. "Trust in the Lord with all your heart." **With all your heart.** Surrender your future to His Providence and Will. Pope Benedict XVI assures us, "Do not be afraid of Christ. He takes nothing away and gives you everything."

How is the Lord's heart breaking in your distrust of Him? What are your fears? Turn to the Blessed Mother and ask her to pray that you will have the courage to say "YES!" as recklessly as she did. As you prepare for the day that the Lord will reveal your vocation to you, introduce the "yes prayer" into your life. Each day before your feet touch the ground tell the Lord "yes." Whatever you have for me, "yes." In practicing this openness to His Will, you will surely experience His Providence in your daily life. You will also be ready to say "yes" with confidence when the Lord discloses the vocation He has in store for you.

I believe people tend to think that priests and nuns spend each day of their lives thinking of nothing but their sacrifice. On the contrary, those living a vocation of religious life find their very joy in this calling. It isn't a lacking that they experience but a fulfillment. Take, for example, a quote from Sister Clare in one of my daughter's favorite Veggie Tales cartoons. While this particular nun is a stalk of rhubarb, I think her sentiment would be echoed by any religious sister you meet. She is asked if she does her work for the Lord to make her happy. She answers with a laugh, "No! I do it because I **am** happy."

Dear HTB,

As you write to your Husband-To-Be this day consider the possibility that the spouse you are writing to is Jesus Himself. Religious Sisters marry a man who is stronger than any you have ever met; they marry Christ Himself. Lean not on your own intelligence, but be ever mindful of the Lord. If you do, He promises to unwind those twisting paths of uncertainty in your life. "He will make your paths straight."

Be honest about your fears and reservations. Write about them and bring them into the light. Ask the Lord to heal you of these trepidations even if He will call you to marriage. Ask Him to continue to open you even further to an intimate relationship with Him as your First Love. Ask for a desire to desire Him.

Tell your HTB you love him even now and that you are honored to wait for him...

*Woman
In
Love*

Chapter 5

All Things New

"For my thoughts are not your thoughts, nor are your ways my ways"

-Isaiah 55:8

Chapter 5 • Woman In Love

Morning followed a sleepless night. Mark had already agreed to drive me to the airport the next day as Christmas Break began. Distressed and confused, I dragged my bags to the lobby of my dorm and waited for the silver two-door to pull up to the sidewalk. The forty minute drive seemed normal yet the pit in my stomach grew. Mark pulled to the curb and exited the car to retrieve my things from the trunk. Not knowing what to expect, I turned to him to express a farewell and found him already returning to the drivers seat. He told me to have a good break, got into his car, and drove away.

Crushed, I made my way to the line of excited travelers heading onward to their winter vacations. At times it seems that the most difficult emotions to cope with are the ones we cannot identify. In hindsight, it is always clear. I had fallen in love with a man who obliterated my expectations, and the only reaction I could offer was utter sabotage. My heart was at war, and my head couldn't interpret the mixed signals.

I didn't eat for the entire day. I made it back to the reality that was my home. As I was drawn into the wild fire, I clearly remembered my reasons for building the wall around my heart. In the month that followed I decided to go ahead and add a few more bricks.

Despite his wounded farewell, Mark continued to call during the weeks that followed. He sent me a care package with a note, a homemade Christmas mix CD and a pair of warm socks. As always, we talked well into the night. Even from a long distance he provided me with a sense of security and peace. As Christmas break drew to a close, the fears began to rise within me once again. What would life be like when I was back in his presence?

It was the night before I was to head back to Ohio. I found myself unloading my uncertainty to my mother. It was a moment that I had longed for, and I discovered the beginning of what would become a great healing between us. I expressed the irony of the agony and utter joy that I received from this man. She asked me a pivotal question. "What if Mark did what you asked of him? What if he gave into your pleas and stopped waiting for you? What if he found someone else, and they began to date and fall for one another?" I was shocked at my reaction. Filled with anger I wanted nothing more than to beat up the hypothetical girl. It was a point of no return. I could no longer ignore the truth. Was I willing to lose Mark to protect myself even if there was a chance that there was nothing from which to be protected?

A few weeks passed as I sorted through this new development. It was the first days of February. Five months of spiritual friend-ship had passed since we'd met in the fall. I still didn't know what lay ahead in the future, but I did know that I wanted my best friend to be a part of it. I found myself in the chapel of my dorm on a gloomy mid-western day. Mark was heading up the hill to join me for the afternoon. I looked at the tabernacle in the simple room on the first floor of my hall. I was terrified but I knew what I had to do. I spoke frankly to the Holy Spirit that day. I told Him that I was ready to do what He wanted of me, but I needed His help. I explained that I didn't have the strength to begin the jour-ney on my own, but if He provided the opportunity I would be willing to take that step.

At that same moment a very conflicted Mark Hartfiel was plowing through the unwelcoming weather and trudging up a steep path from lower campus. The sky seemed to echo his disposi-tion as he bitterly questioned himself, "Why I am walking up this stupid hill in February? I am wasting my time."

Arriving at room 314, he entered and removed his coat. After some moments of small talk, he turned to me and once again took a risk. For the first time since the night on the bench nearly two months prior, Mark asked me if I still prayed about "us." Feeling the rush of anxiety flood in along with the strength of the Spirit, I answered. "Funny you should ask me that today." I proceeded to unravel the revelations of the last several weeks and told him about my time of prayer in the chapel. I expressed my remaining hesitations while simultaneously giving Mark permission to dive into the hope that he had been holding onto for months.

As he left my building that day, he ran in to one of my close friends entering the dorm. She headed to my room and asked why Mark was acting so strangely. She explained that it was as if he was about to fly. I recounted the events of the day as she stared at me in disbelief. She had lived the scenario right beside me and was amazed at the turn of events. I found so much relief in our girl-time discussion. As I experienced vulnerability through the calling of the Lord, I was amazed that it wasn't panic that met me on the other side but freedom.

Prior to this new development, my last official boyfriend was in junior high. I could hardly say that I shared much of my heart with this pre-adolescent significant other. This meant I was pretty much venturing into unknown territory in this new relationship. Incredibly, the transition was hardly noticeable. We knew almost everything about each other, and we were so comfortable in one another's presence. Our platonic relationship set a strong foundation of love and respect. This didn't stem from any prior physical interaction but from a tested and proven friendship. He had already shown me what it was to be treated like a queen long before a romantic relationship took shape.

The evolution of the relationship was not only natural but unhurried. Knowing the weight of the decision, Mark knew that he had a distinct responsibility to guard the heart that was now exposed in order to heal. Over the next few weeks, Mark wrote about this in his prayer journal.

"Lord, Katie finally told me how she really feels about me. Thank you so much. I just pray for your Will. I pray that you make me holy. She

deserves the best. I also pray that we don't mess anything up by letting Satan get in the way. Keep him away from us, Lord. I pray again for your Will and for my deeper conversion.

Father, thank you so much for the development of my relationship with Katie. She is so beautiful to me, and I really believe this relationship is of You. Spending time with her today was awesome. She is finally allowing herself to be vulnerable and to let go of her many fears with relationships. We actually held hands today and held our arms around each other as we walked to go pray to you in Eucharistic Adoration.

I continue to thank you for the growth of our relationship. I pray that you make me holy and pure for her, Father. I am overjoyed with the way things are turning out right now. She is such a blessing to me, Lord, and you get all the glory! Bless her family. Look with favor upon them, Father."

Two weeks after the official establishment of our dating relationship we happened upon February 14th. We began the day with early morning Mass and ended it with a dinner date and a favorite childhood memory of mine, a Monster Truck Rally. While it doesn't suit my girly disposition in life, the monster trucks were nostalgic for me as I remembered watching them with my dad as a child. Dressed to impress, we entered the stadium and stuck out enormously from the rest of our company. We laughed and yelled at the event as I explained the finer points of the races and style competition. The fire-breathing, car-eating dragon monster, during the monster-truck-equivalent of half-time, was particularly romantic and inspiring. After the show we made our way back to campus, and Mark pulled his car into the parking lot of the Perpetual Adoration Chapel. He explained that we began our day by meeting Jesus in the Eucharist and he wanted to end it in the same way. He told me that this would be the model for our relationship. To always begin and end everything we did with the Lord.

Chapter 5 • Woman In Love

Several years prior I had asked the Blessed Mother to help me in my walk toward purity and toward my HTB. I implored her that the next boy I kiss also be the last. I was sure to explain to her that if the Lord had other plans in my search for my future husband and if this request didn't fit those plans then I would understand. That night I looked at this man in a dim streetlight. I heard his promise to surround me with the love of Christ. I felt my desire to reciprocate that undertaking to the best of my ability. Time stopped, and Mark kissed me for the first time. All I could think about was her. The Blessed Mother had heard my prayer and offered it to her Son. I experienced a love that was encapsulated in purity. It was peace and fireworks all at the same time. After a few moments he put his arms around me and asked me if I was okay. I had never been better.

The time that followed wasn't always easy. We learned how to disagree and how to best express ourselves to one another when we were upset. We learned how to spend our time sensibly with respect to each other's daily responsibilities. He learned that I didn't think that wearing thermals under shorts was fashionable. I learned that Mark thought it slightly irresponsible to find unknown cash in the pocket of a pair of jeans. In contrast, I felt that I had made money just by getting dressed that morning. Some lessons were small and easy to surmount, others were painful but powerful to overcome. Many experiences were accompanied by verbal reminders from Mark that he was not my father.

Often times we would continue our tradition of staying up talking while one day turned into the next. We wouldn't want the nights to end. As we sat in his car with the heater blazing on those cold Ohio nights, I was suddenly beginning to believe the expressions that he uttered. Like the prophet in the book of Hosea, he lured me out into the desert and spoke to my heart. He backed up his promises in prayer and in deed.

It was here that I began to experience the healing touch of

Christ. In Scripture, He assures us that He will make all things new. The Lord was accredited to a reformation of my bitter heart. He was replacing hardness with hope. I found myself recreated. You see, it wasn't just that I became capable of receiving love. Christ was giving me the courage to empty myself out and pour myself into another individual. Jesus' Love on the cross was a self-gift. It was an emptying. Christ was pouring this Love into me and allowing it to overflow into Mark. As usual, the Lord didn't use the method that I had planned. He annihilated my expectations by going above and beyond. Without consulting me, God chose Mark as His vessel to save me from myself. I couldn't be more thankful that He did.

YOUR STORY

What is your brokenness? Name it. In the Old Testament, Moses goes to the source of his people's captivity. He approaches the Pharaoh and claims freedom. What is your Pharaoh? Allow your wounds to be exposed in order for the Lord to heal them. God wants to recreate you and make you new regardless of your past. Whether you or another is to blame, lay those hurts at the Lord's feet without delay.

Hundreds of years before Christ's birth the prophet Isaiah wrote, "Can a mother forget her infant, be without tenderness for the child of her womb? Even should she forget, I will never forget you. See, upon the palms of my hands I have engraved you" (Isaiah 49:15-16). Jesus fulfilled this scripture when He wrote your name upon His hands as they were pierced for you. Embrace that reality today as the Lord expresses His desire to recreate a new heart in you.

Chapter 5 • Woman In Love

Dear HTB,

John the Beloved Disciple and Mary the Mother of God knelt together at the foot of the cross. At one of the last moments of Jesus' life, He gives away one of His greatest gifts.

> *"When Jesus saw His mother there and the disciple He loved, He said to His mother, 'Woman, behold your son,' and to the disciple, 'Behold your mother. From that moment the disciple took her into his home."* –John 19:26-27

Jesus held on to his mother until the very last moment. He lifted Himself up on the nails that pierced His hands and feet in order to heave a breath. He gives the Blessed Mother not only to the Beloved Disciple, but to the Church. In this statement, He gives the Blessed Mother to you. He asks that you take her into your home.

Mary is the greatest gift and the greatest champion of purity. Mary was tempted in every way and triumphed. Through God's grace she becomes our ultimate example. She is your mother too, and she wants to teach you how to be a woman. If you don't have a relationship with Mary, now is the time to invite her into your life. Ask her to walk with you on your path to purity.

As you write to your Husband-To-Be today ask him to invite the Blessed Mother into the home that you will share. Describe the characteristics that she envelops and analyze the way that you fit into this description. Explain your invitation to her to help form you into the woman you want to be for your HTB.

Mary served the Lord with utter humility. She was strong and meek. How do you desire to serve your HTB? How do you hope to encounter Christ through your service to your future spouse?

Tell your HTB you love him even now and that you are honored to wait for him...

Woman
In
Love

Chapter 6

Woman in Love

························· ❧ ·························

*"Holy Purity, the queen of all virtues, the angelic virtue, is
a jewel so precious that those who possess it become like the
angels of God even though enclosed in mortal flesh."*

—St. John Bosco

Chapter 6 • Woman In Love

Our story continues as Mark and I arrived at end of the school year, and we both returned to our separate hometowns. It was brutal to say the least. These were the days when cell phone long distance was only free after 9 P.M. and on weekends. I would find myself staring at my phone as I watched the digital numbers move onward from 8:59. My thumb would fly to speed dial in order to hear Mark's voice for the first time that day! The summer allowed us to grow in our communication and appreciation of one another.

One evening stands out in my recollection of that lonely summer. During our daily chat, I felt a sudden inclination to ask Mark about his conversion experience. I had heard the account several times but on this particular night I knew I needed to know the specific date that the Lord had shattered his world forever. Upon discovering the day, I went to the corner of my room and pulled a spiral notebook from a shelf. I turned to the date in my tattered prayer journal as my heart pounded. I knew with certainty that the Lord had something to show me. There it was. I began to quickly read the prayers that filled the journal during that pivotal week of discipleship training prior to my senior year. The very week that I had decided to climb into the trenches as a warrior for my HTB matched up with the date of Mark's conversion to the Lord! I read the prayers of my 17 year old self as I begged the Lord to deliver my future spouse. I asked that should he be struggling with temptation in moral decisions, with parties, or with the opposite sex that the Lord would capture his heart and show him how much more intoxicating life in Christ promised to be.

On the summer night of this discovery, Mark and I found ourselves once again separated by thousands of miles. However, this time God revealed how He had rendered this distance insignificant when He united us spiritually years before. I began to read these passages to Mark over the phone, and we both wept in amazement and thanksgiving. I could not believe that God answered my prayers in this profound way.

MARK'S STORY

My conversion to Christ was the turning point of my life. When I describe a past event, I always preface it by telling someone whether it was before or after my conversion. In essence, I define my life as either before Christ or after Christ. It was the beginning of a completely new life for me. It was not as if I never sinned again, but my life from that moment on was fundamentally altered. My brain even started to work differently. I saw the world through new eyes, the eyes of faith. More than any other single thing, Christ brought so much joy and love into my life. I began to understand the love that God the Father had for me which transformed me. I began to open up my hands to receive His love. This love I tasted from God was better than anything else I had ever experienced, and I began to understand and echo the Psalmist who proclaimed, "For your Love is better than life, so my mouth will proclaim your praise." Because of the radical transformation I personally experienced, remembering my conversion has always been an incredibly joyful and yet emotional thing to do. I am overwhelmed by the way God entered my life and made me a new creation. In general, I am not an overly emotional guy, and I don't cry very often but when it comes to my conversion in Christ, you can throw all of that out the window. I can hardly sing "Amazing Grace" without tearing up because the words define the reality of my life. Truly, "I once was lost but now am found. Was blind but now I see...How precious did that grace appear the hour I first believed."

In context of this profound experience, it is easy to understand why I will never forget the moment I found out Katie was praying intensely for her future husband the exact same week of my conversion. It was one of those few moments in life when time seems to stop; the still-point of life at the intersection of grace and gravity. If you have ever had a such a profound God moment that you feel as if you are not bound to the Earth any longer, then you know what I am talking about. You feel as if the moment has transcended itself.

I always felt a strong sense that someone was praying for me in a major way. Of course, my mother had always been devout and a constant prayer warrior. I am certain that I have received grace from her prayers and love for me, but this was different. The Lord took the prayers of a 17 year-old girl in Colorado, who I did not know, and showered me with grace and mercy. The Lord took her sufferings, joys and faithfulness, and He turned my world around. Years later, he gave us the incredible gift of revealing His Providential plan to us. He opened our eyes to what He had done for both of us. He showed us the reality that Katie's prayers helped transform my life. Nothing could be more powerful!

It goes without saying that I am profoundly glad that Katie was praying for her HTB. If you are ever feeling like there are no good and holy men left in the world to love you the way you deserve to be loved, don't be discouraged and don't lose hope. I was not even close to that kind of man. I was not capable of loving Katie the way she deserved. You could have called me any number of names, but none who knew me well would have called me holy. I can't help but ask what would have become of me if it were not for Katie and her prayers. God is good, and He answered those prayers. Someone somewhere may be in need of *yours*...

YOUR STORY

Now it is your turn. The Lord is writing your love story. Let us start with this scenario: You are having a sleepover with your best friends in the world. The time is in the single digits of the A.M., and you are lying in your room with all of the lights off. As you find yourself stifling your laughter in your pillow, you realize that it is one of those times that it is just so good to be a girl. You dive into the depths of your hearts as the hours melt away. The conversation runs on...

When I describe the above image to the girls that I've worked with, I always end by asking them what the topic of conversation must be. The answer is always the same: boys! Women are expressive and as a result we find so much joy sharing our emotions, analyzing words and actions and generally oozing about the opposite sex with our best girl friends. There is something written within us that urges us to invite others into our experiences and relationships.

I spent many hours living this exchange with my girlfriends before and during my relationship with Mark. In a very real way, they lived my love story along with me. When a woman is in love, she wants to share its greatness with the world! Love changes us... love changed me! True love transforms us into the woman we have always wanted to be and even makes us want to be better than our best! A Woman In Love is swept away by the undertow of something more powerful, more beautiful than she could have described prior to her experience of it.

What if I told you that you could begin to be a Woman in Love this very moment? What if you knew that there was a man who wanted to sweep you off your feet as He waits for you to notice him? What if I told you that you are living and breathing the classic chick-flick plot? You've seen it a million times, helplessly watching as the main character chases after a handsome goon with perfect teeth and flawless hair. Meanwhile her best guy friend, who has secretly been in love with her since kindergarten, waits as the quiet confidant in the background. It usually takes almost the full two hours of film for her to come to her senses and realize that her best friend is also her soul mate.

You see, I think this story is about you. Christ is waiting selflessly as he watches you chase all the things you believe will fill your heart. He is with you, in this moment, anxiously existing in your periphery just longing for you to take notice of Him. He has pictured what your life as a Woman In Love with Him would be like. All He can think about is you. However, He knows that He loves you too much to force this life upon you. He is hoping that you will find out that He is perfect for you so He can show you that you are right.

Jesus literally died to be your First Love. He wants to be the main character in your love story. He wants you to be that Woman In Love. We've all heard the cliché phrase that challenges us to be a "Woman of God." Now of course there is nothing wrong with this title. However, when I personally hear this phrase, I can't help but associate it with long, floral flowing skirts, crocheting, buns and churning butter. In my opinion, I desire so much for you to pursue a life as a Woman in Love with the Perfect Man, your Savior. I long for you to be transformed and carried away by the power of a love that hungers just to be in your presence. I want you to know the joy of sharing it with everyone you know. I hope you will desire to express it with the same eagerness that you will tell of the future love who will put a diamond on your left hand.

To be this sort of Woman in Love is to be a woman of purity. A Woman in Love trusts her lover. If you hope for a true and beautiful, life-giving, real romance with your future husband, you must have Christ as your First Love. If you trust the Lord, and if He calls you to marriage, He will send you a spouse that loves God much more than he could ever love you. My husband knows me better than anyone on the planet, and Christ knows me infinitely better! When I put my trust in Christ, He sent me Mark so that Mark could make me holier. He knew who I needed in order to become the best version of myself. Christ wants to do the same for you. He wants to blow your expectations out of this world and give you the opportunity for you and your future spouse to walk to Heaven together.

Let's stop for a moment and contemplate. What are the qualities that you desire in the man you will someday marry? Surely there are attributes that you are unwilling to bend on. He must be faithful, loyal, trustworthy, fun, honest, ethical and hardworking. Obviously, he will need to be someone that you are attracted to physically and emotionally. Let's take those qualities for granted and stretch your mind and heart a little further. What will set him apart from the other men you have met in your life? Will he be pure, God-fearing, a spiritual leader and a courageous warrior for the truth? Do you desire someone who is chivalrous and wants to fight for your purity? Everyone wants to be able to say, "I've never met someone like him before." What characteristics of an HTB would cause you to utter this statement?

Now picture yourself encountering this incredible man and becoming acquainted with him. Ask yourself: *are you living a life that a man like this would be attracted to?* Would your lifestyle and pursuit of the Lord stand out to a man of this caliber, or would you blend in with all the other girls? What would a man like this list as his priorities in finding a mate? How do you fit that description? You see, the lesson is this: the pursuit of discovering our vocation does not rest simply in finding the man that is best for us. *The journey is also about becoming the woman that the Lord longs to give to a son that He loves recklessly.* We cannot forget that becoming a Woman in Love will begin by letting go of our past self and running toward something better.

We often hear the phrase, "guys only want one thing" as we pass the blame to the opposite sex. However, men would only act that way if they felt they could get away with it. For every guy who gets what he is looking for, there is a girl who is giving it to him. If women begin to demand respect, men will be more inclined to offer it. It is time for a new generation to stand up and help lead men to holiness.

When I was in high school, my mom always told me that I wasn't the type of girl that guys wanted to date... I was the type of girl that guys wanted to marry. At the time, I wasn't a huge fan of this nugget of insight. In my imagination, everyone my age was on romantic dream dates every Friday night while frolicking in fields and the like. Meanwhile I was cozying up with two dream dates of my own: Ben and Jerry. Later on I decided that my mom's observation wasn't so bad after all. I actually came to see it as a compliment. I realized that the boys in my life knew that there was something different about me. It didn't take wearing a t-shirt that said "holding out for marriage" for them to know that I wasn't going to let them use me physically or emotionally. I felt that the guys I knew had a greater respect for me, and I appreciated that. I hoped that one day I would find the man that found my purity attractive. This isn't to say that I did everything perfectly, but I found myself in the midst of the process toward purity. I hoped that I would be the girl he would want to date because he would be interested in spending the rest of his life with someone like me. The Lord was the only one who could bring him to me and satisfy my desires. I wanted to be a Woman in Love.

Someone once asked me if the Lord revealed specific facts about my future spouse during the practice of writing letters to my HTB. Surely the routine convicted me deeply in my devotion to the man I would marry. However, something even more amazing and unexpected happened in the process. I was the one who was revealed. *I discovered less about the essential qualities that I wanted in a spouse and more about the spouse I wanted to become.* God molded me more than He molded my expectations. In fact, the climax of the story came when my expectations paled in comparison to what the Lord had in store for me.

I could have never dreamed up the man the Lord had created with me in mind. As usual, the Lord showed me that His plans are always infinitely better than my own. I have often considered how thankful I am that the Lord chose His own set of qualities for my husband rather than listening to my opinion. Once again, He revealed His faithfulness to me. I had always thought I would have to settle in some aspect of my hopes for a future mate. I had accepted that I would marry a man who was a strong spiritual leader but relatively unattractive to me. I thought the alternative would be marrying someone whose personality and physical attributes were appealing, but who lacked a faithful relationship with the Lord. In response, my Heavenly Father created someone who fit the needs of my soul while simultaneously captivating me on every level. It became clear to me that no woman should ever settle in her choice for a mate. The Lord will always provide in every way and will not falter in His faithfulness. All He requires is our trust.

When we give to the Lord, He returns our self-investment in ways that we could never dream to ask. God will never be outdone in generosity. Your First Love is more faithful than you can imagine, and he desires to give His beloved more than she could ever dream. Yes, your vocation has a name. Whether it be "Bride of Christ" in the form of religious life, or Bride of Christ in conjunction with a Sacramental marriage to another, He wants to give you the desires of your heart, things that you don't even know are there! A Woman in Love trusts her Lover, and her Lover does not disappoint.

We all know that you "can't give what you don't have." I know that you want to love your HTB in the best possible way you can. Yes, often times you will fail, just as we are all less than perfect. Yet, there is a way that you can offer him the best love there is to give. This is when you go to the source. You can't give what you don't have... so I invite you today to turn to Love Himself. Turn to your First Love and ask Him to fill your heart with His perfect love so that you will be able to give it away. The more that you come to know Love Himself, the more strength you will have to love your husband right now, when you look into his eyes on the altar and when you are 80 and holding hands while walking in the park.

Chapter 6 • Woman In Love

Dear HTB,

As you write to your HTB today, tell him about your search for Love with a capital L. Tell him about the Love whose name is Jesus. Tell Him how you want to love God best so that you can love your husband best.

Before you write, turn to the Holy Spirit. Before your pen hits the page, invite the Holy Spirit to rest upon you and your Husband-To-Be at this very moment. Envision this reality in your mind. Breathe Him in with slow deep breaths. In turn, feel the Holy Spirit breathe His Breath on you. In his advice to those returning to daily life after World Youth Day in Sydney, Australia in 2008, Pope Benedict the XVI said, "No one can give what he does not personally possess; in other words we cannot pass on the Holy Spirit effectively or make him [noticeable] to others unless we ourselves are close to Him."

The Holy Father went on to encourage his listeners to remain "within the radius of the Holy Spirit's Breath, in contact with Him. Only if we are continually touched within by the Holy Spirit, if He dwells in us, will it be possible for us to pass Him on to others."

He said that the Holy Spirit can be considered the breath of Christ, and "we, in a certain sense, must ask Christ to breathe on us always, so that His Breath will become alive and strong and work upon the world. This means that we must keep close to Christ."

Reflect on all of this as you write today. Tell your HTB that you want to be able to pass the Spirit on to one another, both in times of struggle and triumph, both before and after you meet.

Tell your HTB you love him even now and that you are honored to wait for him...

*Woman
In
Love*

Chapter 7

Guarding One Another's Soul

"As the pilot of a vessel is tried in the storm, as the wrestler is tried in the ring, the soldier in battle, and the hero in adversity, so is the Christian tried in temptation"

— St. Basil the Great

Chapter 7 • Woman In Love

At the dawn of our relationship, it became clear that Mark and I both had an authentic hunger for purity. Mark was my first "real" boyfriend, and many areas of our relationship were like sailing uncharted waters. Dating someone usually comes with some sort of physical interaction outside of pats on the back or bumping knuckles. In my past I had encountered very few threatening situations when it came to my purity. As I found myself falling deeper in love with Mark, I discovered chastity more difficult than ever before.

Through this discovery the Lord molded our spiritual muscles to become more successful in warding off temptation. Take this analogy for example, Mark has always been an athletic type and spent countless hours in the gym or on the field in college playing basketball, flag football or just working out. Often times, Mark would invite me to come join him while he exercised. I, of course, answered, "You think I'm fat don't you?" This was not a serious reply; however, I did deny his every request to accompany him. I am fairly certain that I am allergic to physical activity. I am more of what you would call an "in-doorsy" type; in general, I find no joy in sports or exercise. Somehow, Mark eventually persuaded me to agree to join him in the gym one evening. I entered the weight room and surveyed the torture chamber of strange equipment. Mark began to instruct me as I lifted some embarrassingly small dumbbells. I watched myself in the gigantic mirror, exposing me to full-on public humiliation. Needless to say, I didn't last long. My first weight lifting session was also my last.

Now, imagine for a moment that I had some enthusiasm in this category and came back the very next day. Perhaps this would have become a habit for me and eventually I could have upgraded to an only moderately embarrassing dumbbell size. My strength would have increased, leading me to lift heavier weights. Eventually I would have been bench pressing my roommates. Similarly, when encountering temptation, we can choose to turn it into an opportunity to build virtue. Yes, it was much more difficult to be chaste with the man I was falling for. However, this battle forced us both to increase our reliance on the Lord to strengthen our chastity. We hoped that one day this would carry into our married life. I remember hearing a chastity speaker explain that when you sleep with someone before marriage, you learn that this person is willing to have sex with someone to which they aren't married. He explained further that every time a couple decides against instant gratification, they increase their ability to say no when temptation arises in any circumstance.

We've spoken so much about the beauty of chastity and it is time to move on to some practicalities. So the burning question arises: How does a Woman In Love, who wants to live chastely, conduct herself when she is in a relationship with a boy? You will be relieved to hear that I will not be advising turtlenecks or parents sitting between you at the movies. However, I do hope to give you some pointers to draw from as you develop your own game plan for purity. Now is the time to make the decisions about your own standards. Don't wait until you are cuddled up with soft music in the background listening to him explain that he "has never felt this way before." If you want to guard your purity of heart and body you must develop a battle plan before heading onto the battlefield. Don't wait until you find yourself surrounded.

The previous chapter was all about trusting in the Lord as your First Love. Has He shown you that He is worthy of this trust? After all, He did piece you together in your mother's womb and infuse a soul into your body. He did incredible things in His life on Earth, including dying and rising from the dead. He hasn't stopped there as He has worked miracles over the last 2,000 years. Lastly, He is the Creator and expert on all things created, and that fact alone should be enough to convince us that God probably knows something about the way we should use our bodies! He didn't send us with an instruction manual, but He does have a thing or two to say to guide us in the right direction.

Chapter 7 • Woman In Love

Often times it seems that the topic of chastity is interpreted as a message of, "no, no, no and more no!" What I want to suggest in the following pages is to the contrary. In fact, **chastity, at its core, is all about "yes, yes, yes!" Yes**, Lord I will trust you! **Yes**, I will use my body to give glory to you! **Yes**, I want everything you have in store for me!" In all actuality, God loves sex. He created it! He could have gone with the stork or the cabbage patch, but God had other plans. In saying "yes" in the context of that gift, according to the intention for which it was designed, we realize just how beautiful it is. By trusting our First Love and following His plan about sexuality, we discover what the devil is trying to hide.

Sex is, in fact, Sacramental. Yes, that's right, I just put the words "sex" and "Sacrament" in the same sentence. The definition of Sacrament is an outward sign of an inward grace. The Sacraments are just one example of how smart God is. He gave us the Sacraments so that we wouldn't miss the mind-blowing things that He wants to do in our lives! It is a way that we get to see, hear, feel, and experience a supernatural reality that is happening within the depths of our souls. In the Sacraments we are given a chance to physically witness a greater spiritual reality.

Each of the seven Sacraments has two parts, their "form" and their "matter." The form is something that is spoken during the Sacrament. An example of this would be in the Sacrament of Baptism. An individual is baptized with the words, "I baptize you in the name of the Father, the Son, and the Holy Spirit." In Reconciliation, it is the words of absolution. In the Sacrament of Matrimony, the couple speaks their vows in order to administer the Sacrament to one another. The matter on the other hand is an action that takes place. In Baptism, this is the pouring on of water. In Confirmation, the Holy Oil anoints the head of the newly confirmed. In Marriage, the matter is the act of sexual intercourse between two people, joining themselves together as one flesh both physically and spiritually.

Wow, no wonder Satan doesn't want that to get out! Who knew that sexual intercourse was actually a moment where a couple receives grace from the Lord! The sexual act within the context of marriage is actually a visible sign of an invisible reality. It is meant to make us holier and it is meant to be a way to use our bodies to give glory to God. In marriage we receive grace through sexual union. All you have to do is turn on your television right now and you will see that the world is sadly missing out on this reality. The devil has succeeded in making sex seem so casual, yet simultaneously making us believe that it is dirty. The average person probably has no idea that there is anything holy about sex. Ladies, it is time for us to stand up and reclaim the truth!

The truth is that there is even a biological reality that occurs when two people join together in sexual union. This shouldn't come as much of a surprise; God did create science along with everything else. Studies have shown that a hormone called Oxytocin is released in excessive dumps during sexual activity.[1] Oxytocin is the same hormone that is dispensed in a woman's brain at the time that she is nursing her new child. It is nicknamed "the bonding hormone" because it literally creates a chemical bond in the brain of a mother. This subconscious connection tells the child and the mother that they belong to one another. During intercourse an incredibly large dose of this hormone is released in the brain creating a concrete chemical bond between two individuals. God's motivation for creating this exchange is simply genius! When a man and a woman speak their vows they give themselves to one another completely for life. The physical reality of this is made present in a biological way when they give themselves to one another through intercourse. Oxytocin is a scientific representation of the Lord's will for the couple to be "no longer two but one flesh" (Mk 10:8). God intended for us to bind ourselves to our spouse. What an incredible gift!

Unfortunately, this isn't always the case. It is now easy for us to see problems arise when the sexual act is taken outside of mar-

Chapter 7 • Woman In Love

riage. The body is speaking a language. It is clearly saying, "I give my entire self to you without holding anything back. I am binding myself to you for life, and I am yours freely, totally, faithfully and fruitfully."[2] The body is saying one thing, but it fails to echo reality. When two people have sex outside of marriage, it literally means that their bodies are lying to one another. While an individual may be able to deceive themselves, they cannot fool biology. I have often encountered couples who are sexually active and continue to break up only to get back together over and over. Their friends can clearly see the relationship is not working, and often it seems that the couple knows it as well! This bond within their brains and their hearts is so strong that even their obvious incompatibility can't seem to break it. When we act outside of God's plan, our vision tends to get blurry.

Perhaps you want to turn now to your Creator and ask for even more insight into His Plan for your sexuality. You can trust Him. This isn't about God telling you what to do or not to do. It is about a Father who wants what is best for His daughter. God wants to provide you with an opportunity to see what incredible plans He has in store for you. He would love to offer you some guidelines to achieving those goals.

Consider an analogy that I once heard connecting this concept to a blow dryer. Most blow driers come with a tag that states, "do not use under water." Why, you ask? Apparently enough multi-taskers out there thought they could wash their hair and dry it at the same time. The manufacturers were then obligated to inform everyone that this is a very bad plan. Does anyone become angry with the company for including this tag? Do you throw up your hands in anger proclaiming, "Who are **they** to tell **me** how to use **my** blow dryer?" Of course not; they have only provided you with this guideline because they made the blow dryer, and they have some insight into how it works. I am sure you are free to use it in the shower if you would like, but the creators would like to warn you that it won't be a happy ending. Perhaps your Creator desires to advise you in the way you use His masterpiece in order to prevent disaster.

When I started dating my husband I knew that there was a strong chance that he would be "the one." I was determined not to jump to that conclusion in haste and reminded myself often how important it was to continue to pray for my HTB. I did however add an additional intention to my prayers. At each instant that I would offer my Husband-To-Be to the Lord, I proceeded to pray also for Mark's future wife. I wanted to be sure that I didn't take any piece of Mark, emotionally or physically, that belonged to her. I cared so deeply for Mark and respected him so much that I really desired God's Plan for his life. I wanted nothing less for him than I hoped for myself. I prayed for her, that the Lord would mold her into the woman he needed her to be and that she would guard his purity. I knew at the time that those prayers would be heard and answered whether I was praying for a stranger or praying for myself.

The virtue of chastity is based on a mutual love and respect for one another, and ourselves, as eternal beings. Even men and women who are married are still called to live the virtue of chastity in the way they approach their spouse and their sexuality. For this reason, living chastity does not just mean not having sex. Likewise, we cannot limit chastity outside of marriage to "not having sex." There are many temptations in a dating relationship that do not fit the strict definition of intercourse. So, here comes the question you have been asking since you opened this book. How far is too far? Allow me to ask you a question in response: why do you want to know? If your intention is to discover how close you can hover around the line between morality and immorality without erring in sin then perhaps we've forgotten the bottom line about what chastity is all about.

Let us not forget what it is to be a Woman in Love. Being truly in love isn't about doing the minimum! It is about finding out

Chapter 7 • Woman In Love

what we can do to exceed the expectations and hopes of our lover. My husband does not just do what is expected of him in our daily lives. Sometimes he makes me omelets while I am still sleeping on a Saturday. Other times he washes and vacuums my car without mentioning it to me at all. This isn't because that is what he is supposed to do; it is because he wants me to know that he loves me. Love isn't about obligation it is about a person. When we set boundaries in relationships, it can never be about pushing limits. Love is about doing whatever we can to ensure one another's safety while we prepare each other for Heaven.

While we keep this in mind, I do want to give you three general rules to help keep those situations in check. In general, if you are feeling uncomfortable enough to ask if you are going to far then you probably are! When discerning these particulars within your relationships consider testing it against the concepts below. All of these insights come from advice I have heard from others along my path toward purity, and I hope they will give you as much freedom as they provided me. These guidelines should help save and free you from those situations and the anxiety that tends to accompany them!

Rule # 1: Don't let anyone touch you in an area covered by a bathing suit manufactured before 1950.[3]

Have you seen those images of the first Barbie in her black and white striped one piece? There is no cleavage and her upper thighs and midriff are covered. Wow, that girl still looks good. This image is so helpful in establishing some great boundaries for Ken and for you.

If you still need some parameters for yourself and your significant other, just remember that neither of you should be touching a part of anatomy that you don't have yourself. Touching these organs has a purpose, and that purpose is called arousal. Arousal is like a giant red LED flashing arrow pointing toward an event that we all know as intercourse. Whether or not that is the intention or the final result is beside the point. Touching these areas of the body are reserved for the Sacrament of Matrimony and rightly so. If he just can't seem to keep his hands to himself, remember the commitment you have already made to keep your body sacred.

Rule # 2: Live in the Light

> *"For you were once darkness, but now you are light in the Lord. Live as children of light, for **light produces every kind of goodness and righteousness and truth.** Try to learn what is pleasing to the Lord. Take no part in the fruitless works of darkness; rather expose them, for it is shameful even to mention the things done by them in secret; but **everything exposed by the light becomes visible**, for everything that becomes visible is light. Therefore, it says: "Awake, O sleeper, and arise from the dead, and Christ will give you light."*
> *(Eph 5:8-14)*

Live this passage. Live in the light. If your mama, pastor, youth minister, friend who can't keep a secret, or Jesus Himself turned on the light and walked in on an intimate moment between you and your significant other, how would you feel at that moment? This verse tells us that light produces every kind of goodness and righteousness and truth, which is exactly what we want in our relationships with one another. It tells us that the works of darkness that are done in secret should be exposed. The conclusion is that we shouldn't partake in anything that you wouldn't want everyone to know about.

This guideline clearly has plenty of implications regarding sexuality, including casting light on soft or hard pornography, touching, overly passionate kissing, masturbation, impure thoughts, inappropriate jokes, and ill-intentioned or inauthentic flirting. Imagine your future spouse, the man you will love more than you could even put your mind around now, more than you think you are even capable of. Picture yourself walking into a room and turning the light on, thereby exposing him participating in the action in question. If you are questioning the moral integrity of a particular expression that you are tempted to engage in, go ahead and imagine how you would feel if you witnessed him doing this with another girl. The conclusion: when we live in the light, we have nothing to fear.

Rule #3: Stand up for what you believe in.

What does it mean to "stand up" for your faith? We generally think that it means to speak out or defend our faith when it is challenged, questioned, or misunderstood. It may also apply to a time that we see someone being abused, mistreated, gossiped about, or being treated unjustly and we intervene by speech or action.

Take this phrase literally for a moment and consider physically standing up for your faith. Often times people talk about getting "carried away" or "caught up in the moment" when it comes to their sexuality. There is some definite biological truth to this. Our bodies are sexual creatures and are programmed toward reproduction. Physical and emotional circumstances trigger physiological reactions. Our brains, hearts, and bodies must work together to stay grounded in a given moment of passion. There may come a time when you need an escape plan. If you find a situation becoming hot and heavy, stand up for your faith. No really, stand up! I am talking about physically standing up. The mood is broken and both of you can regroup and evaluate how you can prevent this from happening again. John Paul II tells the youth of the world:

*"I am sure that you all want to build your life on a solid foundation which will enable you to **stand up** to the trials that will never be lacking – a rock foundation."*

He was right, our trials will never be lacking. We know that having a foundation made of rock is the only way to keep us from being swept away by passion and by the culture. Embrace your purity, live in the light, stand up for your faith and know that you are not standing alone.

Lastly, remember that a Woman In Love doesn't just guard her body, she strives to preserve her heart. Just as we don't want to give our sexuality away too soon, we should also hold on to the purity within us as well. Yes, other people entered both of our lives before Mark and I met. However, it was so clear to me that I was the first one to really enter into the garden of his heart, and he to enter mine. I remember sharing with my friends the certainty that I had that Mark had never loved anyone the way that he loved me.

I clearly recall the day that I began addressing my letters to Mark rather than to my HTB. The decision was of great magnitude! I didn't want to have to tear out a section of my journal if our relationship didn't work out! I wanted to make sure that when I began referring to him by name, it was because I found what I was looking for. While it was unbeknownst to Mark at the time, this moment was a turning point for me in my emotional investment in our relationship. I wrote,

"It's you! I've finally found you. Before I even saw you in class, I was sitting at the Steel Cross and thinking, "I wonder if my husband is here right now, in a dorm room asleep somewhere on this campus and I got chills. I've been praying for you for so long Mark, for years, and God listened because He sent me you. All of those fears and grievances on the pages before this, they've helped mold my standards. You know better than anyone next to God what my fears have been. I'm not afraid with you, Mark. You tell me you love me and I believe you. Miraculously, I believe you. Before this, even up until the time we started dating I couldn't picture someone really loving me. I could imagine myself loving and someone possibly caring about me to a large extent but never that loving-another-as-yourself thing. You amaze me! Thank you for loving me.

I want to walk to Christ with you. I want to bring us to holiness and allow you to draw us there. I know God called us to one another. I want to serve you. Christ said He came to serve rather than to be served and that's the attitude I want to have, serving the Christ in you.

I'm so glad it's you. God doesn't only suffice, He exceeds our expectations.

I love you, Mark. God bless you as always. I'm praying for you still and I'm so glad I don't have to wait to find you anymore."

I praised God that He had finally shown me what it was to be a Woman in Love on every level. He had blessed me with the opportunity to embrace the double meaning of this phrase. Christian author, Max Lucado, once said, "A woman's heart should be so hidden in God that a man has to seek Him just to find her." Truly, the Lord had hidden me that I may be found.

YOUR STORY

I cannot stress how important it is to reserve the intimacies of your heart while you protect your body. As women, we internalize our experiences. We let them sink deep within us. This is a gift. It is also a quality of ours that we must keep in check. When you are dating a Godly man, just remember to remain practical. Avoid the temptation to talk about marriage prematurely, which applies to conversations with your boyfriend and with your friends. Remain realistic about where you are in a relationship, and be sure your heart and daydreams stay balanced with that reality.

Most importantly, don't share your heart with someone that you know you wouldn't marry. In high school my friends and I had a motto, "We don't date just for the sake of dating; we date to marry." Dating has one purpose and that is to discover whether or not this person is a potential spouse. If you know you aren't in it for the long haul, don't give your heart away. If you do, you are only setting yourself up to break up and have emotional baggage in the future.

It says in Song of Songs 2:16, "My lover belongs to me and I to him..." A Woman In Love is a guardian. She recognizes that she belongs to Christ; therefore she desires to be guarded and lives with an eternal perspective. She wants to deliver herself and others to the throne of the Lord. She belongs to her First Love, who gives her the power to execute her mission.

Dear HTB,

Chastity is hard. If it was the easy path, everyone would choose it. If the cross were comfortable wouldn't there be more people carrying it? You have chosen the better part. The rewards will be great, but the struggles will be many. It will be lonely at times. Perhaps you will have to find the right words to end a relationship that isn't preparing you for eternity. Nothing that is worthwhile comes without a price. You are that price.

We decide that chastity is right for us when we have a face attached to it. Suddenly, the struggles are no longer considered a burden. A firefighter doesn't run into a fire for the sake of enduring the flames; he does so with a purpose; and because of that we call him a hero. Whether you choose it or not, the flames of the culture are licking at your feet, and you are called to be heroic in your own battle.

Pope John Paul II tells us that "only the chaste man and the chaste woman are capable of true love" because the chaste man and woman have known the joy of reaching for a goal and attaining it. They have the other's eternal souls in mind and would do nothing to jeopardize that. The true love they possess comes from the fiery Heart of Mercy burning in the chest of Christ. They wear the crown that for many is a burden.

Other struggles will arise in your relationship with your HTB. Tragedy may strike your life as uncertainties lay before you. The virtue that you build before and after you meet your future spouse will help carry you both through the difficulty that is life. The crown of chastity will serve as strength in every part of your life as it teaches you how to love in every way.

The future is unwritten, and all you have is the present. As you write to your HTB today, resolve to live your vows, "for better or for worse..." Tell him about your hope for loving him with the "true love" of which the Holy Father speaks. Tell him you can do anything through Christ and that you want Christ to use him as a vessel. Express your desire to trust him. Let him know that he can trust you. Explain to him that you are working at this moment to be the woman that he can rely on when life becomes difficult.

Tell your HTB you love him even now and that you are honored to wait for him...

Woman In Love

Chapter 8

Guarding One Another's Body

"It is not always in the soul's power not to feel a temptation, but it is always in its power not to consent to it."

—St. Francis de Sales

Chapter 8 • Woman In Love

It was New Year's Eve and I flew to Houston to spend the week with Mark and his family. This Christmas vacation could not have been more different from the previous year's break. I felt I was almost a different person. The Lord had truly taken me back to the potter's wheel and refashioned me. To remove impurities, clay must be vigorously kneaded and pounded. I too had been refined through an intense process. I was now experiencing the beauty that I had once hoped lay at the end of that process of purification.

We planned to exchange Christmas presents at some point that evening. I grew excited as Mark instructed me to get dressed up and bring my gifts along as we joined his parents for Mass. At its conclusion we walked outside the church to find a limousine waiting for us in the parking lot. My heart leapt as I had a feeling I would be telling the story of this night for years to come. We drove to dinner and then spent the evening savoring the sites of Christmas lights while we toured the city. Mark unveiled his Christmas gifts to me, and among them was a book by his favorite author regarding the powerful beauty of the Sacrament of Marriage. On the front was a photograph that he had carefully cut out of the two of us. It was pasted over the cover art, and Elmer's glue oozed from the edges. On the inside he had written to me in the margins, explaining his desire to make me his bride. I was overwhelmed by his musings, and for the millionth time, I wondered how I could deserve this man!

Mark leaned over and turned on the limo's television for the countdown to the New Year. The reception was spotty, so we happily counted backwards in Spanish on the only station we could receive. At the strike of twelve, I found Mark on one knee with a small velvet box in his hand. Everything stopped as he asked me to be his wife. I assume that I said yes, although I have no memory of my response. It was the moment I had longed for since my pen hit the paper and my knees hit the floor years ago. I had dreamed that the Lord would fulfill the desires of my heart. Here before me was my HTB, and I knew this wasn't an end but only a beginning.

Years before, on my 18th birthday, my two best friends pitched in and purchased me a chastity ring. It was a thin, simple, silver band that read "Jesus, I Trust In You". I had worn this ring on the ring finger of my left hand for years waiting for the day that it would be replaced. A new year began that night, and a new ring was placed on that same finger. My old ring represented an anticipated love, while the new one symbolized the fulfillment of waiting. Mark had given me a ring, and I had one to give to him as well. My heart pounded as I explained the importance of my chastity ring and the role it had played in my waiting. I gave it to him and asked him to please keep it safe. I knew I could trust him to continue to guard my purity, and the diamond on my left hand was proof. In his proposal, he essentially asked my permission to make my holiness his mission forever. It was a request I was happy to oblige.

We made our way back to his parents' house to celebrate. It was so fun to call our friends and family and tell the story over and over! Additionally, I couldn't help but be excited to share the news with my HTB in my journal.

"Finally! We're Engaged! These pages are full of anticipation for you! You are my one and only! Praise God! Thank you for my favorite night ever...You're the one I want to come home to every day! Today I found myself envisioning the times I will wait at our home for you to arrive after work. You will come in tired but relieved because it's Friday, and I will greet you at the door. We'll hold each other and just love one another. I'm so excited for those moments! I pray I can be worthy of you. I am praying for a greater understanding and capacity for loving you. I want all the best of me for you, nothing less. I love you, and I'm so glad that I don't have to wait to find you anymore.
Love, Your Fiancé - Katie."

Chapter 8 • Woman In Love

Prior to our engagement, friends and family would often ask the cliché question, "Do you think you've found 'the one'?" For me, "the one" meant that Mark would be "the one" person I would share everything with. My future, my children, my home, my decisions, my finances and my life would all be his as well. However, this also meant that Mark would be "the one" person I would share my body with. It has become more and more clear that the Lord spared us for one another. My husband and I discussed recently how extremely blessed we feel that we have never worried about many of the life-altering issues that keep so many people awake at night. I definitely don't feel as if I "missed out" in any fashion in my pursuit of chastity. We have no regrets. I decided to save my virginity for him, and he did the same for me, long before we ever met one another. How silly would it be to regret that? It is only by His grace and mercy, not my own virtue, that I was spared. I was protected, and the Lord wants to protect you as well.

What does God want to protect you from? He wants to shield you from brokenness, but he also wishes to defend that which He created. Consider the following analogy. My grandmother and grandfather have lived in the mountains of Colorado since I can remember. Each year my family and I take a trip to visit my home state and make a point to drive to their tiny homestead perched on the side of a mountain. Since my childhood, I have loved walking the paths that stem forth from their isolated home hidden in the evergreens. My grandmother usually accompanies us on these expeditions, pointing out interesting facts about our surroundings or telling us great stories about her experiences. My grandmother also packs heat. Yes, my feisty grandma brings her gun on our outings. Her experiences have shown her to be prepared when walking out into the wilderness. All native Coloradans know that when wildlife is encountered, the unexpected can happen. If that animal happens to be a baby expect the risk to increase infinitely. Mother won't be far behind. The last place anyone wants to find themselves is smack between Mama Bear and Baby Bear.

The King of the Universe is infinite, omnipotent, indescribable, untamable, massive, and mysterious. He is also a Father, your Father. He is a doting dad whose favorite pastime is to look upon you and adore you. He is a Father that wants to give His daughter everything and will stop at nothing to do so if she allows Him. Just as a mother bear is willing to do anything to protect her young, our Father will stop at nothing to protect you!

The Lord wants to protect your heart **and** your body. I have always found myself reluctant to discuss sexually transmitted diseases (STDs) within the context of chastity and purity. I believe there is a real temptation to use STDs as a method to scare people into abstinence. I never wanted to use the topic in a manner that wasn't backed by the proper motivation. It wasn't until the Lord recently opened my eyes to the severe and brutal truth of the presence of STDs in our world today that I realized the importance of shedding light on the topic. I literally feel a personal and moral obligation to tell you what you aren't hearing on the nightly news.

First, imagine a world where each person was only sexually active with the person to which they were married. If this fantasy were to begin today, a few generations would pass and eventually STDs would become nearly extinct. Sexually transmitted diseases almost always come from sexual intimacy. They are spread when individuals contract them from one partner and then give them to a different partner. Purity and chastity guard our hearts and also our health. God knows what happens biologically when we don't follow the way He designed for us. He sets up His guidelines so that we won't have to learn that reality the hard way.

In the 1960's, when the "Free Love" age of promiscuity really took off, there were only two known STDs in the world: Chlamydia and Gonorrhea. Viruses are persistent, and the more opportunity they are given to mutate the more prevalent they will become. Today there are more than 25 different sexually transmitted diseases ranging in symptoms and severity. Something has been happening over the last generation. The increase of STDs is related to the increase in non-committal, multi-partner sex in our culture. Sex outside of marriage is becoming a social norm, and as a result, more and more people are connected emotionally and physically. The result of this modern reality is a web of individuals who are sexually exposed to one another and their sexually transmitted diseases. As former U.S. Surgeon General C. Everett Koop has said, "When you have sex with someone, you are having sex with everyone they have had sex with for the last ten years, and everyone they and their partners have had sex with in the last ten years."

It is not my goal to delve into an intense discussion of the disturbing physical realities that each and every sexually transmitted disease brings with them. I am sure your health teacher has plenty to say regarding those details. Instead, I hope to give you a realistic picture of the intense threat someone faces when they engage in sexual behaviors outside of marriage. While there are many, I would specifically like to touch on two of the most prevalent STDs that are successfully attempting to swallow our culture today.

The first of these is the Human Papilloma Virus (more commonly known as HPV) which affects more than 440 million people and is currently the most commonly spread STD in the world.[1] HPV is the virus responsible for 90% of genital warts. It is estimated that in the US there is a new case of genital warts every second.[2] More frighteningly 99.7 percent of cervical cancer is a direct result of the Human Papilloma Virus.[3] In the United States alone, 30 women are diagnosed per day with cervical cancer and eleven die from it.[4] Worldwide 288,000 women die each year from cervical cancer which does not include those who are infected by HPV-inflicted cancers of the anus, vagina and vulva.[5] In our country, the death toll for cervical cancer is roughly equivalent to that of AIDS.[6]

Currently no cure exists for the Human Papilloma Virus.

Often times HPV causes no symptoms for months or even years resulting in infected individuals spreading it unknowingly. HPV can even be passed on to your children years after contracting the virus. This is an incredible concept. A child could potentially be born to suffer the effects of this virus even if the man who infected their mother is from a past relationship. Although there is no cure for the virus, HPV is not permanent. The virus can run its course in an individual and eventually one can be free from infection.

In light of these disturbing facts, we haven't uncovered the scariest revelation yet. The Human Papilloma Virus has become a sexual epidemic. Unbelievably, 80 percent of all women will have HPV at some point in their lives before they turn 50.[7] Currently, 40 percent of all sexually active girls between the ages of 14 and 19 have HPV.[8] Let's translate this into your daily life. Imagine that you are talking to ten of your sexually active teenage friends. This statistic would mean that 4 of them are probably currently infected with HPV. Wow! Let's go ahead and up the ante with one more mind-blowing stat: 46 percent of all teenage girls that do contract HPV will become infected on their *first* sexual encounter.[9]

So we ask, why the popularity of this unwelcome friend? HPV is extremely easy to become infected with. While it is called a sexually transmitted disease, this virus is not passed by sexual intercourse alone. HPV is contracted by skin to skin contact. This means that any area from the thigh to the abdomen can carry and spread the virus and HPV can even be passed by way of the hand. It is alarming to think that someone doesn't have to technically have sex to become infected. Due to its nature, even within the context of intercourse, condoms offer little protection from the spread of this disease. Companies that manufacture condoms do not claim to offer any safeguard from the virus as they are well aware of their inability to provide a level of defense. Like a field that catches fire while in a drought, the blaze of HPV is spreading from one dry blade of grass to another with tremendous speed and success.

Chapter 8 • Woman In Love

HPV is not the only silent prowler in our midst. While HPV is the most commonly spread sexually transmitted disease, Herpes is the most common in terms of people currently infected. Herpes is transmitted by sexual intercourse, oral sex, and can also be spread by way of the abdomen, thighs and hands. When used correctly, condoms are only 50 percent effective in preventing the spread of Herpes.[10]

While Herpes is most famous for causing blisters in your private zone, it also creates a greater risk for contracting and spreading HIV.[11] Additionally, women who have Herpes are also more vulnerable to cervical cancer.[12] Like HPV, there is no cure for Herpes, however, unlike HPV, Herpes is permanent. Once someone has Herpes, they will have it for the duration of their life. While it is uncommon to pass on to your children, it may be fatal for the new-born child if contracted.[13] For this reason, most women who have Herpes deliver by cesarean section.

At a routine appointment with my gynecologist, I overheard the doctor in the exam room next door diagnosing a woman with Herpes. The woman sounded distressed, and she was met with a calm tone as the doctor explained the disease. My heart went out to the woman, as I realized this event probably took place nearly every day in these exam rooms. About one in six of all people is infected with genital herpes.[14] Let's translate this again. We can take six random people in public and most likely one of them will have genital Herpes. By the year 2025 it is estimated that 40 percent of all men and 50 percent of all women will have this incurable disease![15] How in the world could this be true? An estimated nine out of ten people who are infected don't know they are infected.[16] Individuals are altering other's lives forever without even knowing it!

I may not know you, but I can tell you that I care about you. I am praying for you as you read this, and I feel a strong responsibility to increase awareness so that you can be armed against this enemy. Be warned, the rest of the world may not share my sentiment. As we have seen, STDs in our culture have become so widespread that they have practically become the norm for sexually active individuals. In fact, *half* of all sexually active individuals will have an STD at some point in their life![17] Unfortunately, the response from many of those who claim to care about your health is fairly apathetic.

Too many organizations choose an approach that sends a message, which severely downplays the effect that a sexually transmitted disease can have on your life. The Vice President for Medical Affairs for Planned Parenthood, Dr. Vanessa Cullins, nonchalantly states, "In terms of sexually transmitted diseases, expect to have HPV once you become sexually intimate, all of us get it."[18] Many professionals treat the issue as if it is a necessary evil for sexual freedom. We should expect to get a sexually transmitted disease as if this is a normal way of life. Shouldn't we be concerned about the way it will affect our bodies and the fact that it could be passed on to a future spouse and maybe future children? The pain, discomfort, embarrassment and even the possibility of risking our lives aren't anything to worry about? I vehemently disagree.

The irony is that STDs are waging a war on the sexually active, yet the topic is taboo outside of health class. Would you believe that in 2009 roughly sixteen times the amount of people died from STD-produced cervical cancer as perished the same year from the dreaded Swine Flu?[19] During the Swine Flu pandemic, events were canceled, warnings were posted in every public place and constant news coverage increased our awareness and fear. Why wouldn't the same intense warning be given to the public regarding the risk of catching a sexually transmitted disease, which could negatively affect or even end your life? Individuals in our culture must be informed that they are hastily exposing themselves to a health threat each time they engage in extra-marital sexual relationships.

Chapter 8 • Woman In Love

Many experts don't even talk about "safe sex" these days because they know the phrase is extremely inaccurate. Outside of marriage, there really isn't anything "safe" about it. The new expression you will hear is, "safer sex." Imagine if you went up in a plane and prepared to jump out with someone who called their company "Safe-ish Skydiving". Judging by all of the numbers we have seen, this "safer" method isn't working out so well. One is forced to really ask herself whether she is the gambling type when approaching these Russian Roulette-like statistics.

The beautiful truth is that safe sex exists. A free and total gift of self without fear of cervical cancer, warts, blisters, or emotional and physical damage is completely attainable! One of the many fruits of chastity is freedom from ever having an STD touch your life.

Perhaps you are someone who has already been affected by the pains of a sexually transmitted disease. Sin often leaves scars behind, even after our souls have been healed. If you are a person in this situation, I urge you to cling to that cross just as your Savior did. Let Him cry with you and hold you in your pain. Trust that the Lord wants to heal your heart and provide you with the opportunity to love in the future. Christ physically bore the evidence of our sin on His body to bring a greater good into the world. Similarly, He longs to use your suffering to mold you in a greater good if you choose to allow Him.

We know there is a greater reality than just the physical one that we see on a daily basis. God created the world so we could see and experience the spiritual truths! We have all felt it when looking at an exceptionally beautiful sunset or watching the rays of the sun shine through the clouds in just the right way, almost as if inviting us to climb them up to Heaven. In those moments, you ask yourself how anyone could refrain from believing in God. Similarly, the intense love that we are meant to feel for and express to our spouse should point us to something that is literally out of this world!

How tragic to look at a world being torn apart by sexual immorality and witness God's desire for the physical expression of love being cast away by so many!

The physical ramifications are vast, but what about the heart? Since the onslaught of free love outside of marriage there has also been a dramatic increase in broken families. Roughly half of all marriages are ending in divorce and 80 percent of people who cohabitate, or "live together," before they are married end up divorced.[20] Hearts that have been bound to another individual through sex outside of marriage are being shattered. A baby is violently torn from the mother's womb every twenty seconds.[21] Obviously the path our culture is taking isn't working. We can try "safer sex" to perhaps deter the physical consequences, but it is true what they say, "there is no such thing as a condom for the heart."

YOUR STORY

God gave us our sexuality, and He wants you to give it back to Him through giving it to your future spouse. God really is an all or nothing kind of a guy. He didn't go to the cross and give only *part* of Himself. In fact, He was beaten severely, carried his method of torture and death, and hung from three nails while his lungs slowly collapsed so that he would eventually suffocate. However, Jesus didn't stop there. The Scriptures tell us that after His death the soldiers came upon his body and saw that He was already dead. Taking his spear, one of the soldiers thrust it into Jesus' side piercing his heart. Blood and water came pouring forth as a stream from His body. When Jesus had nothing left to give, including His life, He physically emptied out His heart for you. Jesus gave it *all*.

It is easy to think of the Lord as someone examining us from a distance without really being able to relate to our lives. On the contrary, He lived it. He paved the way for us to do the same. When the Lord gave you your vocation, He desired for you to walk to Calvary with Him. He wants you to console Him by receiving the gift of His blood washing over you upon His death. The end result isn't death but Resurrection. He wants to give you this free gift and you can give it back to Him by glorifying Him through your life.

Our sexuality reflects this truth. The Lord wants all of you. He asks you to trust Him when He asks you to chastely protect yourself both physically and emotionally, as you follow Him on that all-or-nothing road.

Start with some quiet reflection. We have learned that straying from God's path can lead to ailing bodies, hearts and spirits. Again, Jesus gave it all. Ask the Lord what parts of your sexuality may be holding you back from giving everything to Him. Ask Him what emotional fears or hurts are hindering you from letting go and surrendering.

Write to your future spouse today and allow yourself to be vulnerable to him. Tell him what you are afraid of. Express your desire to give everything to the Lord by giving everything to your HTB. Explain which things will be hard to let go of. What are your insecurities that you cling to for safety? What uncertainties for the future make you anxious? Tell him that by the time he is reading these letters that you want to be "all in." Let him know that you will always have struggles and that when God wills for him to share them with you, you will be ready to let him.

Tell your HTB you love him even now and that you are honored to wait for him...

Woman In Love

Chapter 9

Modest is Hottest

"Similarly, women should adorn themselves with proper conduct, with modesty and self-control, not with braided hairstyles and gold ornaments, or pearls, or expensive clothes but rather, as befits women who profess reverence for God, with good deeds."

– 1 Timothy 2:9

Chapter 9 • Woman In Love

The years of waiting for my Husband-To-Be to arrive were often brutal. I would reflect on the strange feeling of "missing" someone I had never met. In meeting Mark, and becoming engaged, we discovered that the act of waiting is somehow always present in our lives. We prayed for patience in the months leading up to our wedding. The excitement tempted us to wish the days away. In the midst of this struggle, we strived to live in the moment and express our gratitude for this period of our relationship. I loved being engaged. The best part of this experience is the fact that you don't go through it alone. My best friend shared his engagement with me as we both prepared for this Sacrament. I wrote to my HTB attempting to capture in words the amazing sentiments of my heart.

"Mark, you are my vocation. The vocation stamped on my soul, from the moment God thought of me, will help carry us to eternal life. You! It's you! Love wants to overflow out of me, to burst forth! How can I contain this? It has changed my outlook on life and transformed the person that I am."

"I was thinking of how to describe what it is to be in love. Of course, it is a mystery that I cannot explain, but I want to try. Mark, you make me happy to be alive. You make me excited for every stage of life. I would dread certain events in life, but I can now look forward to them with joy. You make me want to be holy. I want to have greater faith primarily to glorify God and secondly to know Love more in order to love you better."

The excitement about our engagement was often hard to contain. I tried so hard to pace myself in conversation in hopes that my friends wouldn't tire of the topic. I spent every free moment searching online images of cakes and floral arrangements as others would poke their head over my shoulder and give their opinion. Wedding planning can be contagious, and soon every friend, co-worker and family member of mine was thrown full-throttle into the process. The only thing better than planning your wedding is doing so with the people you love. It was so affirming to see the joy in others as they shared in my happiness. I became a bride-to-be and everyone I knew associated me with the pending big event.

So it should be with any Woman in Love. Our lives should make it obvious that we are consumed by something exhilarating. If we truly desire to be Women in Love, our outward demeanor must coincide with our inward conviction. The individuals in your life should be convinced of your heart's position due to the expression provided for them. When Mark and I became in engaged, I suddenly found myself beginning to understand the concept of modesty. I wanted to keep my body sacred for him in all ways, including the wandering eyes of others. Perhaps even more so, I desperately wished that other women would refrain from tempting my Husband-To-Be. Suddenly, I began to notice the scantily clad more than ever. I often wanted to apologize to Mark for the actions of my gender.

My conviction was solidified one weekend when we found ourselves walking in the mall. As we passed Abercrombie and Fitch, we were assaulted with a nearly naked woman plastered on a gigantic sign. Mark looked at me and commented, "You know, it's crazy. I don't know this woman's name or anything about her. However, I have seen more of her body than I have of yours and I am going to marry you." Wow. It was so obvious, yet I had never thought about it that way.

Alright girls, buckle up. For most of you this will be the most challenging part of this book! A woman of purity challenges men in their faith, but doesn't challenge them to be faithful. According to the type of man you are trying to attract, modest is truly hottest. The struggle that men have with our clothing (or lack thereof) is one that we as women will never fully comprehend. Consider the concept of PMS. Men can't understand it, but they just have to live with and accept it as a reality. Similarly, we have to do our best to make ourselves aware of their battle even when it doesn't add up in our female brain. Let's do even better than that. Let's rise up and aid them in their victory!

We'll start with the root of the problem. Ok, yes, the male body is attractive to women. However, rarely does it consume our thoughts and lives in a way we would call threatening to our own holiness. It is no news that men and women are created utterly and fantastically different. Our brains are literally hardwired so distinctly that they create an incredible blend of insight and talents when they join together. This concept is no different when applied to various topics relating to sexual relationships. One major difference to address in the discussion of modesty is the male's reaction when seeing flesh. Men's vision is factually drawn toward skin. Scientifically, at climax, a cocaine-like chemical substance is released in the male brain that serves to "addict" them to an image of a woman.[1] God made them this way. In the proper context, a man is meant to bind himself to the beauty of his wife in a way that is pure and inexpressible by words. When taken out of the marital relationship, this astonishing reality becomes perverted and disoriented. Something that is such a gift becomes confusing and crippling. We have the capacity to help restore men's desire for this gift through our example to the men in our lives.

While I was deeply passionate about chastity as a teenager I found myself defensive when it came to the challenge of modesty. While I despised the bikini-clad girls flaunting the cover of male and female magazines alike, I was blinded to my own lack of virtue in this department. I didn't see a problem with the belly shirts, tube-tops, miniskirts and shorts that barely hid my underwear (yes...it was the 90s). My closet and I had a special bond and it was one friend with whom I wasn't yet willing to part. Not until I was in a relationship with my future husband did I connect the dots. I finally understood the attention I was subconsciously requesting and accepting from other men. It was then that the proverbial light bulb illuminated over my head. I knew I needed to shape up and ship some of my fashion faves out.

At last, I heard the words that Jesus had been speaking to me for so many years! Matthew 5:27-30 tells us:

"You have heard that it was said, 'You shall not commit adultery.' But I say to you, everyone who looks at a woman with lust has already committed adultery with her in his heart. If your right eye causes you to sin, tear it out and throw it away. It is better for you to lose one of your members than to have your whole body thrown into Gehenna. And if your right hand causes you to sin, cut it off and throw it away. It is better for you to lose one of your members than to have your whole body go into Gehenna."

Wow! That sure does widen that well beaten path paved with sins of lust. I used to think that men's problem was exactly that, their problem. Why should I have to adjust my actions based on someone who lacked the virtue to control himself? I realized later that when I invite the sin that Jesus is speaking about in the quote above, I become a participant in the sin itself. Suppose you know someone who struggles with alcoholism. Imagine that you bring him to a bar because you don't want his struggle to dampen your social plans. An even more extreme example would be talking to a friend who is suicidal and then leaving them alone with an armed weapon. Obviously there is a responsibility attached to your involvement in these end results! So it is with modesty. If our clothing causes someone to sin "it is better to...throw it away." We have to weigh the cost. Isn't it better to make a small sacrifice and lose a fashion opportunity "than for your whole body [or someone else's] to go to hell"?

Moreover, the thought of becoming the object of a man's sexual struggle is not an attractive thing to me. Several years ago, I found myself at a surprise birthday dinner for a friend of mine. The meal was drawing to a close, and none of the other party-goers were ready to end the festivities. I was early in my first pregnancy at the time, and my body (which was busy making another human) was pretty exhausted and ready for bed. In spite of this, I somehow found myself riding along to a nightclub accompanied by rap music and bright lights. I stood on the edge of the dance floor drinking my Sprite on the rocks and witnessed the scantily clad girls bust their best moves. Across the way I spotted an older man, maybe in his late fifties, smirking as he too observed those whose clothing and actions were shrieking for male attention. My already weak stomach turned in disgust. I had a worldview alteration at that exact moment. I never ever wanted to be on the other end of that look. Thinking of this strange man was disturbing enough, yet envisioning a younger man or someone I knew didn't comfort my queasiness in the least. I made a resolution at that moment to be conscious of my appearance and the power I held.

YOUR STORY

We may not be able to control men, but we can control ourselves. It is impossible to wrap our feminine minds around the male brain. It is understandable that we find it difficult to apply this to what we see in the full length mirror. The truth is that many of our current fashions are literally more revealing than clothing worn by prostitutes in the 1950s.[2] We must therefore develop a critical eye when it comes to our choices. Remember, while other girls are advertising their need for attention, your goal is to advertise that you are a woman of purity while still looking good in the meantime. Bear in mind that you are at a huge advantage considering you aren't dealing with 1990's options for style! You can bust out your maxi dress, layered tee, cowl-neck, pencil skirt, wide-leg, tea-length, boat-neck, cut-too-low-just-throw-a-cami-under-it styles and be mega-cute and mega-modest all at the same time.

The man you are hoping for isn't looking for your curves- he is looking for your soul. What will set you apart from the crowd? You may be tempted to throw yourself onto your bed and flail your limbs as you complain that you "just have nothing to wear." Before you run out and purchase every muumuu on the market, we should talk about some pointers that can be applied to your current dresser. Head to the mirror and give yourself the following rundown. Let's find out if your HTB would appreciate the way you guard his eyes and the eyes of other onlookers!

1. Throw those arms up and praise the Lord girl! Can you see any skin showing in your tummy region? If so reach for a longer layer. It will elongate your torso and be more flattering anyway!

2. Head for some good light. Can you see anything that you want to be kept private? Can you see through your top or skirt? Reach for your friend the cami and grab a slip. Don't have a slip? I bet your mama does!

3. Keep your bra straps a mystery. No one needs to know what color or brand you have hiding underneath. Let strapless be your friend.

4. Try things on with the shoes you are going to wear with the outfit. Heals have a way of making your legs longer and more attention grabbing. (What other reason would Barbie have for walking on her tip-toes all the time?) They also consequently have a way of making your skirt shorter. Add in a stiletto-factor if you are braving the heals. In general, dresses, skirts and shorts should rest no shorter than two to three inches above the knee.

5. Be ready for anything. Sit down and see if your underwear make an escape out the back. Check out your shirt while bending over to make sure nothing is revealed in the front. Check appropriate skirt length by sitting down and crossing your legs.

6. Be aware of your endorsements. No celebrity advertises a product that would jeopardize their image in the eye of the public. Be attentive of the phrases written on your clothing...does it represent you as a Woman in Love with Christ? Be especially conscious if that phrase is located on your behind. It is best to leave that area

blank to avoid generating inappropriate words and thoughts by men. I always feel awkward reading people's butts. It seems stranger to me that they somehow want me to.

7. Save the backs and shoulders for the appropriate setting, especially if you are heading to Mass. Spaghetti straps and strapless have a place, and it isn't in the pew. Grab a quarter-length cover up and throw it in your purse or car if it's too hot to wear during the drive to church.

8. Too tight is just not right. If your shirt or jeggings/yoga pants/skinny jeans make you look like you have denim or spandex for skin, be assured they do not fit into the modest category. Keep your curves a mystery by choosing a silhouette that can keep a secret. Additionally, please remember that leggings are not pants. If something is too short to wear without leggings, it is too short to wear with them alone.

9. When heading to Mass, remember that you will be attending what the Book of Revelation calls the Wedding Feast of the Lamb of God. Dress in a manner that expresses your recognition of this. I would have been offended if someone "dressed down" for my wedding. When you go on a date, you try to look your best. How much more should you "dress to impress" your Savior? I guarantee that you will notice a change in your own disposition during Mass if you outwardly recognize its beauty.

10. If in doubt, don't wear it. I can't tell you how many times I look in the mirror on my way out the door, question one of the above things, come up with an uncertain answer and sigh as I head back to my closet. It certainly does take the challenge up a notch. If I don't know if something qualifies, back it goes. I would much rather feel confident in my clothing than spend all day questioning it.

Paradoxically, all of this has one single purpose and that is freedom. When we feel good about ourselves and our outward appearance reflects that, we find the best kind of freedom. The way we outwardly present ourselves is a reflection of our interior self. That is what fashion is all about! Our motives shouldn't be just to impress, but to express. When we communicate humble and genuine self-confidence in our standards it is attractive. We know that Jesus was a boy once too, and he loves you and thinks you are more beautiful than any other boy ever could. His love letter to you says "Put on then, as God's chosen ones, holy and beloved, heartfelt compassion, kindness, humility, gentleness, and patience" (Col. 3:12). That being said, I think I would take Jesus as my stylist any day.

Dear HTB,

"To defend his purity, Saint Francis of Assisi rolled in the snow, Saint Benedict threw himself into a thorn bush, Saint Bernard plunged himself into an icy pond. You, what have you done?"
-Saint Josemaria Escriva

Love is a sacrifice. Sometimes this means watching an action film when you are really in a romantic comedy mood. Other times it means giving someone else the bigger slice of cheesecake. A mother sacrifices her body in labor pains in order to give her children life. In the ultimate example, we see a man's bloodied body nailed to a cross. Gift of self isn't always easy, but it is always worth it.

Modesty is just one way that we are challenged to let go of our attachments in order to purify ourselves for Christ. In the quote above, Saint Josemaria lists several Saints who inspire us to go to extreme lengths to protect that which is eternal. The beautiful virgin Saint Lucy plucked out her eyeballs and gave them to a man who complimented her on their beauty. After the Lord miraculously restored them, the man converted to Christianity. What do you need to pluck out of your life in order to draw closer to the Lord? Don't underestimate these sacrifices and the affect they can have on other's lives.

In prayer today, ask the Lord what He would like you to remove from your life. Remember, God is never outdone in generosity. Anticipate His gratitude. Expect Him to use this sacrifice to apply grace in your own life and the lives of others. What keeps you from purity? Is it your clothing, music, TV shows, movies, friendships, etc? Are you willing to make a sacrifice in the name of Love?

Pick something to offer as a sacrifice for your HTB. Make the sacrifice of love. Trust that the Lord will take this gift and in turn offer grace to your Husband-To-Be. Maybe it is something that needs to be purged from your life indefinitely. On the other hand, perhaps it is a favorite indulgence or habit that you will give up for a week or two. You may not know the effects of the outpouring of this grace until Heaven, but you can be assured that it will happen!

In your journal, disclose to your HTB that which you will be surrendering and offering up for him. Tell him your motivation for making this sacrifice. Describe your conviction that God will be moving in his life as you offer yourself in this process. Picture it each time you offer something up for him. Explain that every time you are tempted to give in to that which you forfeited, you will offer a prayer and remember your love for him. A sacrifice without love is empty. Take each opportunity and make the sacrifice worth it.

Expect the Lord to reveal Himself to you through your gift. Look for the ways He will be working and journal about these experiences during the following weeks.

Tell your HTB you love him even now and that you are honored to wait for him...

Woman In Love

Chapter 10

Total Gift of Self

"God blessed them, saying: "Be fertile and multiply; fill the earth and subdue it…"

-Genesis 1:28

Chapter 10 • Woman In Love

The best fairy tales end with a Prince and Princess being whisked away by their carriage toward "Happily Ever After." From the time young girls are exposed to this magical imagery, they begin to imagine themselves in a white dress on the arm of Prince Charming. We've pictured running through rose pedals as trumpets play in the background. Planning my own version of the storybook wedding was just plain fantastic. Stacks of catalogs and magazines littered my room. From measuring yards of tulle to hot-gluing centerpieces, my friends and I vigorously embraced every task that came our way. Besides the obvious preparations for the ceremony and reception, Mark and I began a spiritual journey toward the Sacrament that would change us forever.

As I anticipated the biggest day of my life, I experienced times when my nerves would spike. I was getting married…yikes! However, I always found peace in a self-reminder that I wasn't just getting married, I was marrying Mark Hartfiel. He was the one who always calmed my fears. I was not simply going to be a wife; I was going to be Mark's wife. Post-engagement, my letters to my HTB would often begin with the countdown to the day that I would become a Mrs. I had speculated about married life for years, and it was suddenly becoming so concrete.

"I am so excited about the future with you. You are going to father my children, make sacrifices for them, cut their grilled cheese in fours, drop them off at school, tickle and laugh with them, cry with them, watch them sleep, cuddle on the couch with them, teach them how to pray and how to love. We are going to learn from loving our babies. OUR babies. Little people who will come from us…It is so close. It is so concrete and so real."

"You make me want to have children. I want that visual reflection of how much we love one another. I want to look into someone else's eyes and see you and me and a little bit of mystery looking back at me. A new person will grow and affect other's lives because of our love. I want that, not just for me but for us. I want the daily life of wife and

mother. I never knew I could find happiness in these things.

"I had some revelations this weekend about the workings of God. His all encompassing plan, bringing good out of every evil and using those goods as building blocks to a greater good were all made clear to me. During my senior year, my dad told me that he wouldn't allow me to go to Franciscan for college. Part of the fruit of my dad's departure was that I made it to Ohio. The greatest purposes of that struggle are you and the lives we will one day bring into this world. This will hopefully mean more souls in Heaven. That's what marriage is for, right? It's a preparation for a greater good, so even our relationship is a building block for something more!"

The transformation continued as the caged girl of my past became more of a stranger to me. We prayed about our future and made plans for the life we would soon share as one. The Church who had always mothered us was eager to once again take our hands and prepare us for the outpouring of grace that was to come. We met with our Deacon on several occasions. We attended a retreat for engaged couples. Surprisingly, our favorite experience of Marriage Preparation was our Natural Family Planning classes. One Friday per month, Mark and I would join several other couples for an extensive class regarding this gem of the Catholic faith. Following the class, we would relish in the brisk spring evenings as we sat on a bench surrounded by the rolling hills of campus. Accompanied by the illumination of a lamppost, we would rehash the amazing lessons we learned each week. The fruits of chastity had been so apparent in our dating relationship, and we were eager to experience them in our marriage as well.

In recent years I have had several opportunities to share the message of chastity with hundreds of girls. Shockingly, they are always surprised to hear that chastity is a virtue that is critical both before and ***during*** marriage. Remember, chastity is about a mutual respect for the power of sexuality. Our constraints don't fly out the window after the wedding. On the contrary, chastity within marriage is just as important as chastity outside this Sacrament. Chastity helps the married couple exercise an other-centered attitude toward sexual intimacy rather than a self-serving incentive.

Within the vows of the Catholic Ceremony of Matrimony, the priest asks the bride and the groom if they will willingly accept children from the Lord. This is an essential aspect of the marriage. Their answer and the intentions behind it are powerful enough to render the Sacrament valid or invalid because the family is, by definition, an analogy for the Trinity. In the Trinity we have God the Father, emptying Himself completely into the Son. The Son responds by emptying Himself fully into the Father. Their love is so intense that this exchange of self-gift begets another being, God the Holy Spirit. In marriage, a man empties himself into his wife and she does likewise. This love exchange is so intense that nine months later, you have to name it.[1]

A common practice that impedes this creative power in both marital and extra-marital relationships alike is the use of contraceptive methods which cancel out the above analogy. In 1968, Pope Paul VI wrote an encyclical entitled *Humanae Vitae* in response to the societal pressures on the Church to condone artificial contraception. Here he defined contraception as any action that renders procreation impossible in anticipation or completion of intercourse.[2] This would include the pill, condoms, "pulling out," sterilization, and other barrier methods.

Many people, Catholics and non-Catholics alike, fail to understand why this issue is so important to the Church. Once again, we look to the Lord who has fashioned us and likewise invented sex. This entire book has been centered on trusting the Lord and His plan and design. Contraception uninvites and excuses the Lord from this aspect of a relationship. When we contracept in a sexual relationship we obstruct the physical ability to conceive a child, therefore simultaneously barricading God's creative power. Sex speaks a language, and the act itself shouts, "I want all of you and

I give you all of me!" Contracepting within the sexual act says, "I want all of you, but not that part! I want to give you all of me... except for this!" It no longer becomes a total self-gift, but rather a partial gift. Contraception is, at its core, a deliberate violation of God's design, not what the Lord created but rather an imitation of the real thing.

Until the 1930s, all Christian denominations held the same stance on artificial contraception. By the time Pope Paul VI wrote *Humanae Vitae*, the Catholic Church was the lone advocate against the issue. In his letter, Pope Paul warned his readers about the consequences that would surely follow should contraception become a widespread practice. He prophetically predicted a rise in infidelity in marriages, divorces, a loss of respect and objectification of women, and a general lowering of morality. Obviously, these predictions have surely come to pass. In removing the creative power from the sexual act, intercourse is reduced to merely a pleasurable act. The result of this is a slippery slope toward an attitude that sex is a self-serving activity. In disregarding the spiritual aspect and regarding sex as a selfish desire, it is easy to see why the results would be just what Pope Paul VI predicted.

You may be one of the many girls who is on the pill but not sexually active. Your reason may be due to acne, painful periods, or irregularity. Every time I discuss this issue with young women they become very concerned that they are sinning in a grave way. The answer is simple. If you are taking birth control, but are not having sex, then you are not contracepting. Your usage of birth control is not impeding pregnancy. Therefore, it is not sinful. However, you should know that just because the pill is widely prescribed doesn't make it healthy. The danger lies in the fact that the pill elevates estrogen levels in non-pregnant women which can cause a number of serious medical problems. This is especially true if it is taken over an extended period of time.

Furthermore, people don't realize that the pill and barrier

methods of contraception act as abortifacients, which means that when a birth control method fails to prevent an egg and sperm from meeting, fertilization takes place. As a result the pill and barrier methods keep this new life from attaching itself to the uterine wall which is essential for survival. We, as Catholics, believe that life begins at conception. In this moment a soul is infused into a new eternal person. If a fertilized egg cannot attach itself to the uterine wall, it will exit the body at the next menstrual period, thereby causing a technical abortion.

So what are we to do? Surely we aren't expected to conceive and bear a child every nine months? Remember, each time we see the Lord offering a guideline steering us away from something that is bad for us, we also see His gentle hands steering us toward something that is beautiful! Natural Family Planning is a safe and healthy practice that brings freedom and virtue into many areas of marriage. Natural Family Planning (commonly referred to as NFP) uses the cycle that the Lord designed in order to predict when a woman is fertile. This technique helps couples to achieve pregnancy when the timing is right and avoid pregnancy if there is a genuine reason to do so.

Here is how it works. Every woman has a unique cycle that functions under three phases. Phase one is the time that a woman is menstruating. Phase two is the time in the middle of the cycle when pregnancy is likely because the environment of the body is favorable to bring forth life. Phase three is the period of time after ovulation when the window for fertilization is closed. NFP uses signs such as temperature and physical indicators to help a woman reveal where she is in her cycle. Husband and wife, together with God, can then determine when it is time to engage or abstain from intercourse depending on their intentions.

The natural consequences are a greater understanding, appreciation and awareness of one's body. Furthermore, NFP is a huge opportunity for couples to communicate and continually pray about the plan that the Lord has in store for their family. Each month of charting these signs opens a door for couples to talk and plan. The virtues of self-control, chastity, respect, obedience, and temperance definitely overflow into every aspect of the relationship. From finances to child-rearing and everything in between, a couple who practices NFP benefits from the good habits they develop.

I remember attending Mass as a child at my home parish and noticing a particular family who would always sit a few pews ahead of us. While I didn't know them personally at the time, I could always see something special in the way they interacted. It was clear that the mother and father truly cared for one another. I could never quite pin point the reason for this conclusion, but I could see the love of this family radiating from them. As the years passed, we became acquainted with them and over time became friends. Their oldest daughter and I started to spend time together, both in and out of our high school youth group setting. Her parents, Dan and Amy, welcomed me into the loving environment of their family. My sense that there was something distinctly special about this family was confirmed. Dan and Amy's relationship and love for their children was exactly what I wanted for my future. As things fell apart in my own family, my yearning for this life I witnessed in their home grew ever stronger.

During our Natural Family Planning class, my questions about Dan and Amy were finally answered. For years I had seen respect, communication, love, admiration, consideration, generosity and responsibility exhibited in their relationship. Consequently, these values came alive in their daughters as well. As we sat in our classroom on campus, I remembered that Dan and Amy taught NFP to engaged couples in Colorado. When I arrived home for summer vacation, I met with Amy to ask her some additional questions. I divulged my secret admiration for them and explained my revelation. She confirmed the blessing that Natural Family Planning had been to their lives. She too felt that she could look at a couple and see the fruits of NFP in a relationship. How unfortunate it is for so many couples to miss out on this incredible opportunity for their marriage and family.

However, like all good things, numerous myths surround Natural Family Planning. I am so thankful for the opportunity to dispel these myths to you as, sadly, you may have few chances to hear this beautiful message again in the culture in which we live.

Myth # 1: Natural Family Planning is Catholic Contraception

On the contrary, where contraception effectively removes God from the equation, NFP factors Him right in. NFP should never be used to solely and indefinitely prevent pregnancy, but rather, to plan along with the Lord according to His design. Natural Family Planning uses the cycle that He gave us in order to allow us to walk with him in discernment.

Consider this comparison. Say you have two friends that are both trying to lose weight. One friend becomes bulimic and engorges by indulging herself in binge eating. She then causes herself to vomit in order to prevent the food from making her gain weight. The other friend develops a scheduled exercise routine and a healthy diet of foods. Both friends lose weight. One friend wants the pleasure of food without the natural effect. The other friend uses food and exercise in the way her body was designed to process it. One friend deserves congratulations, the other friend needs help. The goals are the same but the means couldn't be more different. So it is with the comparison of Natural Family Planning to artificial means of contraception. One method uses the body's God-given abilities while the other distorts them.

Myth #2: It doesn't work

On a personal note, I can tell you that NFP has worked beautifully for us since our marriage. It has fulfilled its promises for family planning. We spent years prayerfully discerning the timing of each of our children and NFP did its job both in delaying and achieving our pregnancies. When Natural Family Planning is practiced as designed it is 99 percent effective in delaying pregnancy.[3] This is the same claim given by manufacturers of the most popular form of artificial birth control: the pill. You may have heard Catholics talk about their unplanned pregnancy and blame Natural Family Planning. Mark uses a phrase that I love, "NFP doesn't fail people; people fail NFP."

When I was engaged, a woman who worked with me told me, "Katie, I have one piece of advice for you when it comes to Natural Family Planning. I've learned that when the chart says no…the chart means no." Our NFP teachers explained that they were almost always able to interpret a chart from a month that resulted in an unplanned pregnancy in order to pinpoint where the human error occurred. They concluded that a true "surprise pregnancy" that was unexplainable in terms of what was recorded on a chart was extremely rare. Birth Control has the same disclaimer. All artificial methods of contraception advertise that they must be used as directed to be effective.

Myth # 3: It's just too hard

For many people this seems to be the turn-off for practicing Natural Family Planning. They seem to think that abstaining during the fertile period is simply impossible. I, however, tend to think that people are being a bit too dramatic when they make this assessment. In fact, while it can be difficult at times, the phase of fertility can be an incredible opportunity to express your love in alternative ways. NFP keeps the romance of communication and quality time alive in marriages.

Furthermore, this is the perfect time to recognize the way that premarital chastity can influence your married life. A couple that exercises chastity outside of marriage has no problem applying that same self-control within their marriage. A married person can use the self-restraint they learned in preparation for marriage within the Sacrament itself. Couples who practiced abstinence before marriage will naturally have the ability to say, "This isn't what is best for our relationship right now."

Lastly, Natural Family Planning is marriage insurance. The divorce rate in America is somewhere between 40 and 50 percent.[4] However, the divorce rate for couples who practice NFP is only an estimated 5%.[5] Natural Family Planning provides the temperance and self-control to abstain from your significant other when the timing isn't right. Similarly, it helps to annihilate the temptation for infidelity in marriage. The Catechism of the Catholic Church puts it best when describing Natural Family Planning: "These methods respect the bodies of the spouses, encourage tenderness between them, and favor the education of an authentic freedom."[6] Respect, tenderness, and freedom, these words sum up the essence of Natural Family Planning. They also represent exactly what the Lord wants you to discover in your marriage to your HTB. Never sell yourself short on the plan He has for you!

YOUR STORY

The Lord has something incredible for you. He wants to offer you the whole package. He doesn't want you to miss a thing. Take, for example, the pre-school-sized princess kitchen in our playroom. It is overflowing with all sorts of dining delights that my daughter loves to prepare for us. We have tea and pie on a regular basis, often several times a day. The food looks realistic and the burners even make boiling sounds when the tea pot is placed upon them. However, we know that while these plastic foods resemble the real thing, they are only imitations.

Why settle for an impersonation in your faith life when you

can experience the real deal? Following God's plan for our relationships, in and out of marriage, is the sure path to the full experience. In John 10:10, Jesus says that He came "that [you] might have life and have it to the full." He didn't say He wanted you to have life to the half. He wants to give you everything! There is no exception when it comes to your vocation. He designed an incredible plan for you and He hopes that you will come to find the joy He desires for you!

Dear HTB,

One of my favorite things to write to my HTB concerned my fantasies about our spiritual life together. I imagined walking in the Communion line with him behind me. I told him that I couldn't wait to sit beside him and pray after receiving the Lord knowing that Christ was truly dwelling physically within us. I would picture what it would be like to pray in front of the Blessed Sacrament. I explained my hopes for the conversations that we would have about our faith.

Allow yourself to daydream about these things as you write to your future spouse tonight. Describe your perfect date. Muse about the conversations you will have. Express your desire to share your body, mind, and soul. Explain what that will look like. What do you hope "life to the full" will look like alongside your mate?

Lastly, discuss your opinion on the topic of contraception. Describe your willingness or struggle to follow the Church's teaching. Express the ways that you see this concept applying to John 10:10.

Tell your HTB you love him even now and that you are honored to wait for him...

Woman In Love

Chapter 11

Transforming Mercy

"Create in me a clean heart, O God, and put a new and right spirit within me."

— Psalm 51:10

Chapter 11 • Woman In Love

By now I hope you have been convinced that your heart, your soul, and your body are worth protecting. It is clear that The Lord gave us our sexuality in order to give Him glory. If He calls you to marriage as your primary vocation, you will receive many gifts from friends and relatives. Mark's favorite aspect of wedding planning was definitely the gift registry. We would enter the store and approach the guest services department in order to be handed the seemingly magical scanning gun. I was not allowed to scan anything myself, as Mark was too intrigued by the power that lay beneath the trigger. Aisle by aisle, we would discuss the differences in blenders and towel sets until we agreed on a particular item. Every time we left, Mark would comment about the thrill of shopping without spending a cent.

The gleaming white wrapping paper, ribbons, and bags that stack up at your gift table during your dream reception will only be a symbol of what is to come. Earlier, we defined the word "vocation" as "total gift of self." Spiritually, emotionally, and physically you will truly become a gift on your wedding night. Picture that gift in your mind at this very moment. Imagine the most beautiful parcel you could possibly dream up. The creases are perfect, the paper is intricate, and the ribbons and bows are tied in such a fashion that you couldn't possibly decipher where they begin and where they end. For analogy's sake, let us pretend that this present represents the incredible gift of your sexuality. This is the gift of all gifts, which you will one day give to your husband. For now, it is in your safe keeping.

Perhaps you reach, or have already reached, temptations that threaten this gift of your sexuality. Maybe you have struggled with impure thoughts toward the opposite sex. Giving in to this temptation may be equivalent to tearing a small amount of paper from the side of your perfectly packaged box. It is possible that maybe you have gotten a little too passionate while kissing someone and allowed your body to kick into overdrive. Suddenly some tape is ripped from the side. Inappropriate sexual jokes, pornography, oral sex, masturbation, petting and touching, grinding and sexting all begin to dent, bang up, tear and damage the perfectly crafted gift. Envision yourself handing this gift to your husband on your wedding night with the cardboard box showing and bow untied. No, the box has not been unwrapped and unpackaged, but the damage is undeniable.

Maybe you are someone who has already neglected to care for the gift of your sexuality. Maybe you have been reading page after page and wishing that you had chosen differently in your path to purity. If so, this message is specifically for you. Our God is a God who keeps His promises. Jesus Himself looks to you this day and utters the words that He spoke in Scripture, "Behold, I make all things new" (Rev. 21:5). St. John Vianney tells us, "The good Lord is more eager to pardon a repentant sinner than a mother is to rescue her child from the fire." Your First Love, and the one who knows and loves you perfectly, desires to look into the eyes He created as a window to your soul. He wants to gaze at you like a lover and see the brokenness that lies within your heart. Like a knight to the lady in distress, He wants to save you from all that threatens your ability to be one with Him. Yes, truly, He wants to forgive and make all things new.

Because you see, He didn't come to take that package and tape it back together. He didn't shed His Blood so that He could retie that bow and fix what has been wronged. The Lord made Himself present in the Sacrament of Reconciliation so that you could come and whisper into His ear. He designed this incredible opportunity so you could physically hear your failings and watch them be swept away by the words of absolution. St. Therese says, "All possible crimes, [are like] a drop of water thrown into a burning furnace."[1] Before that drop can even meet the flames, it is obliterated. Yes, the Lord came to make all things new, and He doesn't offer you a gift that has been repaired. The Lord, who created you to begin with, longs to hand you a new gift just as perfect and alluring as it was before. The mercy of God knows no limits. It is infinite.

Chapter 11 • Woman In Love

Consider the example of the Prodigal Son in Luke's Gospel. His sins are many, including sins of impurity. Chapter 15 verse 18 says, "I shall get up and go to my father..." He says this with confidence. He doesn't doubt that he will find mercy. He continues, "...I shall say to him, 'Father I have sinned against Heaven and against you." As the son is arriving home, the father is waiting for him. We can imagine that the father has done this every day since his departure. Each morning he would arise and make haste to set his eyes on the horizon. He was longing to see his son's face and offer forgiveness. "While he was still a long way off, his father caught sight of him, and was filled with compassion. He ran to his son, embraced him and kissed him" (Lk 15:20). No matter what you have done, the Father will renew the feast of the Prodigal Son each time that you return home through the Sacrament of Reconciliation. In fact, as Saint John Vianney says, "God's greatest pleasure is to pardon us."

In my discussions with young women who have fallen in their past, they often express that they don't deserve a pure man of God as their Husband-To-Be. This statement never fails to shatter my heart. This disposition is nothing but a lie. Mark often explains how Satan will make a sin look like it is no big deal when we are considering committing it. Upon its completion, he then tempts us with a belief that it is too big for God to forgive. Satan's plan is to rob our joy and lead us into despair. Christ nailed that temptation to the cross when, clothed with all the sins of humanity, He turns His gaze to the Father. With every sin on His shoulders, He does not hide His face from God. He does not despair. Christ has taken our sins, every one of them, and has risen from them all. This is our faith. This is the good news of the gospel. The love and mercy of God wipes away all sins and despair. It is never too late to accept this mercy into your own life and become a fundamentally new person in Christ. When we fail to accept the Lord's Mercy, we pain His already wounded heart. Know that you are worthy. You, personally, are so worthy that He died for you. Don't believe the lies of the evil one. God does not desire mediocrity for you as a result of your failings. The Lord could never love you less and He starves to adorn you with blessings just as the father did for his prodigal son. Never settle for a lie because the "truth will set you free" (Jn 8:32). If you are worthy of the Lord's love and mercy then you are worthy of your future HTB's love and mercy. The Lord desires to give this gift to you! He desires your joy.

This new gift consequently becomes in and of itself a symbol of God's goodness. We must remember however, that when we sin it may become easier to fall backwards into the same mistakes. One of the punishments of sin is that we become enslaved to it. At every point in our journey, our shield must be raised to protect and guard our purity from harm. We should never take God's compassion and mercy for granted! God's goodness and faithfulness are immeasurable, and His Mercy is incomprehensible. It is true that when we sin, we are not breaking a rule- but rather, breaking a heart. The Lord wants us to give our all and do our very best. He wants us to run to Him without fear when we fall.

It is incredibly important to realize that we cannot stop here. If you are called to marriage then the man that you will eventually marry is out there somewhere. Yes, he needs your prayers on this journey, but he also needs you to prepare yourself for the moment that he enters your life. We have established that our current culture is a warzone where there are casualties and injuries each and every day. We have all made mistakes regarding our purity. Yes some are bigger than others. As scary and hurtful as it is to ponder, it is important for you to ask yourself the question, "What if?" What if my HTB has made mistakes? What if he has been intimate with other girls? What if he has given himself away to another?

I know what you are thinking, because I thought it often myself. Ouch! What a painful reality to face. Obviously, we hope that this isn't the case, and I assure you that I have heard many stories about couples who have been virgins on their wedding night. It is possible, and it is our greatest hope. However, it is important to ask, "what if?" I think that is when we ask ourselves what we **really** believe about God's Mercy. If you truly embrace that the above is true, can you love enough to trust it is true about your HTB as well?

In my musings to my future husband, I gathered the courage to address this very question. I asked, rather begged, the Lord to show me how to approach the topic. It came down to a simple question: was I a true follower of all that Jesus preached, or was I a Pharisee? Did I believe that the Cross held the power to change people in a radical way? The writer of most of the New Testament, Saint Paul, was formerly responsible for sentencing Christians to death. One of the greatest Saints in theological teaching, Saint Augustine of Hippo, fathered an illegitimate child before his conversion. Matthew the tax collector, King David the adulterer, you and I are all examples of individuals who have been dramatically transformed into new creations. It is easy to look back to the girl who existed before my encounter with Christ and to feel as if she were a stranger to me. I had to ask myself, do I really believe? Do I really believe in God's Mercy? Do I believe that He can cure the sickness within my future spouse and know that he is a new creation?

For me, the resounding answer to all these questions was and is "Yes." I believe the love and mercy of God can transform. I am grateful that God had prepared my heart. Mark's conversion to the Lord came after his high school years, and he was far from perfect. He had given in to modern temptations that teenagers still struggle with today. At the same time, it was clear that the Lord had preserved him and his heart in many ways. His total gift of self remained, reserved for his bride-to-be. We had discussions pre and post wedding regarding this topic, and one comment that he made will always stick with me. Mark explained that our body naturally makes and replaces our cells constantly in our youth. Any girl who exfoliates knows the importance of ditching that dirty old skin in order to reveal the new skin that lay beneath. He told me that in his own healing from his mistakes, he found comfort knowing that in a real way the old Mark was gone. The new Mark was here to be a gift to me.

To state the obvious, this doesn't mean that you should date a man who is currently living impurity while you hope to change him. Remember that we talked about the importance of never settling in your search for a man of God. Your relationship shouldn't challenge you to justify your beliefs, but should be a catalyst for bringing you closer to Christ. If, however, your significant other has a past and longs to leave it behind, you should be an instrument of the mercy of the Lord. Alone, this concept is crazy and unreasonable, but with Christ, it is powerful. Let Christ infuse His Love within you so that both you and your HTB can be cleansed.

YOUR STORY

Where is your Husband-To-Be right at this very moment? Let your mind run wild with possibilities. Maybe he is the same age as you, or maybe a few years older or even younger. Allow yourself to wonder what stresses him out and what makes him laugh. Speculate about the number of siblings he has and his relationship with his parents. Furthermore, what are his weaknesses and temptations in life? How does he need your prayers?

Before I met my husband, I remember being very discouraged by the world around me and the men I found in it. Honestly, for a time, I became pretty bitter toward the male gender. I wondered if there were any holy men left out there. I painfully came to realize that perhaps my HTB wasn't making the same choices toward purity as I was for him. I knew that he and I would have a pure relationship with one another and all of these things would be far in the past by the time we were married. I had to ask myself if I would be able to love all of him, including his mistakes. It was then that I really had to face the truth about what I believed

Chapter 11 • Woman In Love

love to be. I had to ask if I would be able to offer the same forgiveness that Christ would hand him freely in the Sacrament of Reconciliation.

"I glorify You in making known how good You are toward sinners- that Your mercy prevails over all malice, that nothing can destroy it, that no matter how many times or how shamefully we fall, or how criminally, a sinner need not be driven to despair of Your pardon."
-St. Claude de la Colombiere

I would lie in bed at night and wonder where my husband was at that very moment. I would rage in battle as I prayed and begged with everything I had. I chose to be a lover and a fighter. I asked God to preserve him in the purity he maintained and save him in the places he struggled. I fought for him and I fought for me. I wanted to be the woman who really believed in the power of the forgiveness of Christ, not just talked about it in theory. I wanted to embrace it as someone who needed it but also as someone who wanted to give it away.

Dear HTB,

Pray today for your future husband wherever he is. Pray for his struggles, big or small. Pray that he is waiting for you. Pray that if he isn't, God will work a greater good and that you will both be transformed because of it. God has done many more amazing things than this.

As you write to your HTB tonight, tell him your fears about his path. Allow yourself to work through this process with him in your journal. Let him know that you are asking God to transform you as well as transform him. Describe your desires for the life that chastity will bring to your relationship. Explain that you know he will love you like he never knew he could love anyone. Be confident in your love for him, his love for you, and the overwhelming love of the one who will bring you together. Saint Josemaria Escriva tells us: "When you decide firmly to lead a clean life, chastity will not be a burden on you: it will be a crown of triumph." You will be your husband's queen as you bear this crown in your life together.

Tell your HTB you love him even now and that you are honored to wait for him...

Woman In Love

Chapter 12

Your Reason

"*Therefore, since we are surrounded by so great a cloud of witnesses, let us rid ourselves of every burden of sin that clings to us and persevere in running the race that lies before us while keeping our eyes fixed on Jesus, the leader and perfecter of faith…*"

- Hebrews 12:1-2a

Chapter 12 • Woman In Love

Nothing in life is like the freedom of summer as a small child. Days wind in and out in a carefree rhythm of bug spray, lemonade and sunscreen. One of my favorite memories of childhood summers is walking to the ball field in my oversized cap and mitt ready for an exhilarating tee-ball season. I was an outfielder, which meant little action considering the lack of sluggers under the age of six. I spent most of my time looking for animal-shaped clouds and four-leaf clovers on the field. Of course, the best part of tee-ball, next to the popsicle and juice box at the end, was my turn to bat. It was in this experience that I realized the reason for the phrase, "Keep your eye on the ball." My heart would pound as I approached the plate. I would put my elbow up and swing with all my first-grade might. As my bat neared its target, my gaze would shift toward the centerfielder expecting an out-of-the-park home run. More often than not, one of two things would happen. I would either strike the tee knocking the ball a few feet in front or I would completely miss the ball and the tee. It was time to learn that I needed a specific place to put my focus if I wanted results.

The spiritual life isn't much different. If you have a desire to succeed in your walk with Christ, you must make a decision to "keep your eye on the ball." You have to find a "why." Why do you want to be pure? Why is it important to you in a world that doesn't place much value on chastity? Why wait for later when you can satisfy a temptation now? It is my hope that in taking this journey together your "reason" has revealed itself to you in a profound way.

In a world where we are assaulted and distracted by crude speech and poor examples from both other individuals and the media, we need a plan in order to "keep our eye on the ball." In God's love letter to you, He lays out the means to victory. Saint Paul tells us in Hebrews 12:1-2, that if we want to rid ourselves of every burden of sin that clings to us, we have to persevere in running the race. He goes on to explain the key: to keep our eyes fixed on Jesus; to have a reason.

When I talk to young women about their choice to be pure, I cannot place enough focus on this element of the pure life. I ask them to define the reason for their decision to be pure. I explain to them that the time to discern their answer is right here at this very moment. As we've said before, no army enters a war without a clearly formulated motive for victory. Today is the day.

As a teenager and young adult, I realized that my reason was not a "what" but a "who." I knew that my future spouse was out there. I wanted to give my total gift of self to him and him alone. However, while this fact was a pivotal part of my drive toward purity there was someone stronger thrusting me forward. I knew, and still know, a man that I love much more than I love my husband. My primary reason is Christ. Your reason should center on protecting the heart of your First Love. Wherever you are on the path to purity, I know that the Lord is running to your rescue.

It was the day before my wedding, and every sentiment one could imagine was rushing through my veins. A perpetual to-do list played in my mind as last minute touches sprouted upon it. Evening approached and the tasks dwindled while everything began to fall into place. Guests were escorted from the airport, and the reality of what lay ahead began to take hold. With the decorations, rentals, timelines and pick-ups confirmed, only one thought remained. This was it. It was my last night as a single woman. Tomorrow I would take on a new name, a new role and a new life. Just one week prior I had penned one of my last letters to my HTB:

"Writing these letters always puts me in awe of the miracle we are to one another. It's just after midnight which means one week from today we will be one. I have been anticipating this for many years... the day this book will find itself in its owner's hands. That person is you! During this past year, I have felt so many emotions: nervousness, impatience, excitement, and peace. Right now, in this moment, all I am experiencing is a genuine happiness. I know I am meant to feel

this amazing delight and tranquility as I anticipate the mystical occasion that will occur so very soon: our Sacrament of Marriage. I will be yours and you will be mine. I love you, and I pray to love you better. God bless you. I'm always praying for you!"

Exhilarated, I arrived at the rehearsal. I saw my Husband-To-Be standing in the same church where I was cleansed in Baptism, first encountered the Lord's mercy in Reconciliation, received my First Communion and was Confirmed in the Spirit. Joy and serenity overflowed. This face was the one I had waited for. This face was the one I wanted to look upon every day of my life. It was the face I hoped would motivate me when I labored for a child, the face I wanted to cry with, the face I wanted to laugh with and the face I wanted to watch age as the years passed us by.

The night rolled on and the rehearsal, dinner and toasts came to a close. Our guests continued to socialize, but Mark and I stole a few moments alone at the hotel before parting. The evening felt surreal for many reasons, but none compared to what I was preparing to do. My heart pounded with disbelief as I handed him a package containing that which was most precious to me. Mark opened the gift and revealed a simple three ring binder with a handmade envelope attached to the front. Confused, he looked my way for an explanation. Filled with emotion, I instructed him to open the envelope and read the letter. With my head on his shoulder I read alongside him as he came to understand the magnitude of that which he held in his hand. At the time, neither one of us would have ever dreamed that this letter would one day become the first page of this book.

As his eyes met mine, I saw into the window of his heart. In an instant it was all clear to me. Everything was worth it! The heartache, the pain, the anguish, the fear, the healing, and the triumph washed over me all at once. All of these things had drawn me to this one moment. Filled with gratitude I praised God for his faithfulness. He had promised me a fulfillment of the desires He placed in my heart, and He did not disappoint. I knew with utter certainty that I wouldn't change the past for anything. I had been molded into a Woman in Love, but not just any Woman in Love. I had finally become the woman that the Lord wanted to give His son on the following night.

Yes, I realized these things about Mark, but God revealed to me how much greater this encounter would be with Him one day when I transition from this life into the next. Just as I have no regrets about my decision to wait and persevere in purity for my HTB, it will again exceed my expectations when my eyes look into my Savior's for the first time. I imagine these exact same words only now about Love Himself...*As His eyes meet mine I will see into the window of his Heart. In an instant it will all be clear to me. Everything was worth it! The heartache, the pain, the anguish, the fear, the healing, and the triumph will all wash over me at once. All of these things will have drawn me to this one moment. Filled with gratitude I will praise God for His faithfulness. He has promised me a fulfillment of the desires He placed in my heart and He will not disappoint. I will know with utter certainty that I wouldn't change the past for anything.* This indeed is the ultimate love story and this love story is meant to be for each and every one of us no matter what becomes of our love life on earth.

Just minutes before midnight, I said goodnight to Mark and knew that the next time we laid eyes on one another it would be through a tunnel comprised of the gazes of everyone we knew and loved. Their eyes would follow as I walked the journey down the aisle to my Husband-To-Be. I would meet him at the end and he would unveil his bride. My wait was finally over, and the rest of the story was waiting to be written...

Chapter 12 • Woman In Love

YOUR STORY

In ancient times, a female child was given a dowry upon her birth to be saved as an offering to her future spouse on the occasion of her marriage. This item served as a perpetual reminder of the gift of self she would offer her husband. It was always something of value and considered one of the prized possessions that a young woman owned. For many Jewish families living 2000 years ago, this dowry came in the form of a box made from a precious stone, alabaster.[1] Within the box was an expensive perfume used for anointing. When a woman married her husband she would break the box at his feet and anoint him as a symbol of her years of preparation. It was a moment of outpouring and self gift.

All four Gospels include an account of a woman who approached Jesus with an alabaster box of perfumed oil which she used to anoint the Lord. In Luke's description we find Jesus dining with the Pharisees when a sudden unexpected guest arrived.[2] She approached Jesus weeping and fell at his feet. She adoringly breaks this jar of oil and anoints him.

This unnamed woman sees the opportunity before her to run to her Messiah and offer Him her everything. I would imagine that she had heard Jesus speak or just heard the stories that others were telling about Him and that her heart was set ablaze. In her desperation to express this fire that her bones could hardly contain, she hastily sought out the most valuable item in her possession. Without fear, she entered into a public figure's house, threw herself at the feet of a man she had never met, and offered Him a gift that could not be replaced.

Jesus doesn't disappoint. It is in giving herself to her First Love that she begins the voyage of the rest of her life. Surely the moment was pivotal for her, a decisive turning point that dictated her every step from that day forward. She had given Jesus a gift that couldn't be returned, and she showed no regret.

At the breaking of her alabaster box, this woman gave Him her past and her future. What would you risk if you threw yourself at the feet of the Lord? What are your fears? What are you holding on to? Has Jesus ever let you down?

The Pharisees smirked and whispered about the sinful woman's actions, and Jesus rose to her defense. He offered her gratitude in the face of the Pharisee's worldly criticism. He explained that she had anointed him, washed his feet with her tears and then dried them with her hair. As she continuously kissed the feet of the Lord, He raised her face to His own. With a look that penetrated her very soul, He wiped away all of the uncleanliness that He found with His gaze. He accepted her priceless gift, and He returned with something much more incredible. He looked at her and spoke: "Your sins are forgiven you."

I cannot even begin to imagine the emotions that Jesus experienced in this moment. His heart must have leapt with the same power that exploded creating the stars in the Heavens. Jesus became her reason for everything. Are you willing to break that alabaster box at the feet of the Lord? Will you give Him your everything so that He can perfect it and provide you with something infinitely more incredible? Will you allow Him to look deep within your soul and wipe you clean? What will happen if you do?

Dear HTB,

"Blessed are the pure of heart, for they will see God" (Matt. 5:8). A friend of mine once told me that she pictured herself running toward Jesus on her path of life as fast as she could. She would then continue on to envision her future husband doing the same thing. She figured that eventually they would run smack into one another, pick each other up, and run to Jesus together. I often thought of this image during the years before I met my husband. The temptation was to spend my time running toward so many other things, including my HTB, rather than keeping my eyes fixed on Christ.

Blessed Mother Teresa tells us, "To be pure, to remain pure, can only come at a price, the price of knowing God and loving Him enough to do His will. He will always give us the strength we need to keep purity as something beautiful for Him." This price is one we gladly pay for the joy of seeing His face and finding His face hidden in the eyes of our vocation.

As you write today, unveil with utter honesty the areas in which you struggle to keep the Lord first. "But seek first the kingdom of God and his righteousness, and all these things will be given you besides" (Matt. 6:33). Ask the Lord to reveal to you the distractions in your life keeping you from Him. Make a resolution to put Christ first in all things. Promise your HTB that you will do your best to put him second and the Lord first in your life. Beg him to do the same. Explain to him that you don't want to love him with your own love, but with the perfect Divine Love of Christ. Express your deep desire for each of you to drink deeply of the love of Christ so that you can lavish one another in it forever.

Tell your HTB you love him even now and that you are honored to wait for him...

Epilogue

Epilogue • Woman In Love

Katie - My Queen,

Oh my goodness! God has done great things for me. I am totally swept off my feet by your letters. I bet I am the only man in the world that has received so many letters of love. It has taken me seven years to read all of these. I read them slowly because I did not want to be done reading them, ever. Praise Him! I cannot write or say anything that does any justice to the way I feel. Only a **Woman in Love** with Christ and consumed by the Holy Spirit could express herself, preserve herself, and love me the way you have.

Thank you for loving me for all these years. Years when I did not even know you and you did not know me! I was lost in this world, and Christ suddenly and providentially came with power into my life. Thank you for praying for me. Thank you for waiting patiently for me. Thank you for trusting in me.

I cannot believe you would choose to love me so much. It blows me away! I pray that I may open my hands, my heart, and my soul to receive that love from you. Receiving love from you means that I am receiving Jesus from you. It is a spiritual communion and nothing less. I truly love you from the depths of my being. You are a queen. I long to love you more deeply and more perfectly.

Your purity beckons me to a deep, deep conversion of heart. How could someone receive such a love and not be transformed? Your love and purity inspire holy desires within me. I want to be holy. I want to take the love that has been showered upon me and shower it upon you.

I hope that others will find this love that we share in their own lives. I hope that more and more girls will value their purity and save themselves for their HTB. I hope that they will intercede on behalf of their HTB. I pray that God will raise up men who value such women and in turn live lives of purity themselves. I hope that there will be countless men who receive a notebook of letters from their fiancée the night before they get married. They will see how much they are loved and have been prayed for. They will cherish their wives forever.

I want girls to know that when they live lives of such deep purity and love that it will indeed transform. When the man that God has for them comes along, he will be captivated by this purity, and it will be utterly beautiful to him. He will be just like me in the sense that he will look into her eyes and be struck by something incredibly moving and inspiring. He will long to rescue her from this world and any past wounds. He will long to make her happy. He will long to preserve her purity. He will desire to grow in holiness so that he is capable of loving her in the way she deserves. He will lay down his life for her as Christ laid down His life for the Church. He will stand in the place of Christ to be her bride on Earth until the day that Christ reclaims His bride in Heaven. He will never forget how superabundantly blessed he is to have such an amazing woman. A Woman In Love with Christ. A Woman In Love with him. He will be a very rich man indeed. He will have found a treasure.

Katie, I am going to keep loving you more and more each day. Together we will walk hand-in-hand to God our Father. I will walk with my love to My Love.

No longer your HTB,

Mark

Chapter 1

1. Saint Joseph Edition of the New American Bible (New York: Catholic Book Publishing, 1991)

Chapter 7

1. Mary Beth Bonacci, Real Love (San Francisco: Ignatius Press, 1996) 32.
2. Christopher West, Good News About Sex and Marriage (Cincinnati: Servant Books, 2000) 20.
3. Bonacci, 188.   "

Chapter 8

1. "What is HPV" Chastity.org. n.d. Web. Jan. 2012.
2. "Genital Warts" gardasil.com. n.d. Web. Jan 2012.
3. "Human papillomavirus is a necessary cause of invasive cervical cancer worldwide" .ncbi.nlm.nih.gov. National Center for Biotechnology Information, 1999. Web. Jan. 2012.
4. "Genital Warts" gardasil.com, n.d. Web. Jan. 2012.
5. "Cervical Cancer" iarc.fr. International Agency for Research on Cancer, . , n.d Web. Jan. 2012.

6. Miriam Grossman, M.D., Unprotected (New York: Sentinal, 2007) 15.

7. "Human Papilloma Virus" idph.state.il.us, Illinois Department of Public Health" n.d. Web. Jan. 2012.

8. "What is HPV" Chastity.org. n.d. Web. Jan. 2012.

9. Ibid.

10. "Four Top Herpes Transmission Facts You Must Know to Prevent Spreading Herpes" best-herpes-treatments.com. n.d. Web. Jan. 2012.

11. "What is HPV" Chastity.org. n.d. Web. Jan. 2012.

12. Ibid.

13. Ibid.

14. "Genital Herpes" cdc.gov. Centers for Disease Control and Prevention, n.d. Web. Jan. 2012.

15. "STDS/STIS" ashastd.org. American Social Health Association, n.d. Web. Jan. 2012.

16. "What is Herpes" Chastity.org. n.d. Web. Jan. 2012.

17. "STD Information" livestrong.com. Jul. 2009. Web. Jan 2012.

18. "Let's Talk About Sex" bvwellness.com. Nov. 2009, Web. Jan 2012.

19. "Pandemic (H1N1) 2009 - update 100"who.int. World Health Organization, May 2010. Web. Jan. 2012.

20. "Sociological Reasons Not To Live Together" leaderu.com. Leadership University, n.d. Web. Jan. 2012.

21. "Constitutional Amendment 'A Fortress' Against Abortion" priestsforlfe.org. Priests For Life, n.d. Web. Jan. 2012.

Chapter 9

1. J. Reisman, "The Psychopharmacology of Pictorial Pornography – Restructuring Brain, Mind and Memory and Subverting Freedom of Speech", 2003.

2. Colleen Hammond, Dressing With Dignity (Rockford: Tan Books and Publishers, 2005) 51.

Chapter 10

1. Scott Hahn, First Comes Love (New York: Doubleday, 2002) 46.
2. Paul VI, encyclical, Humanae Vitae 14.
3. John and Sheila Kippley, The Art of Natural Family Planning (Cincinnati: Couple to Couple League, 2000) 3.
4. "Divorce Rate: Divorce In America" Divorcerate.org, n.d. Web. Jan 2012.
5. Kippley, 245.
6. Paragraph 15 Catechism of the Catholic Church (New York: Doubleday, 1994) 2370.

Chapter 11

1. Father Jean d'Elbee, I Believe in Love (Manchester; Sophia Institute Press, 2001) 57.

Chapter 12

1. Debby Jones and Jackie Kendall, Lady In Waiting (Shippensburg: Treasure House, 1995) 3.
2. (Lk 7:37-50)

Mark and Katie Hartfiel were married on December 31st, 2004. They currently reside in Houston, Texas where they are both active in ministry. They are blessed to have two daughters with which to share their life and faith.

Did You Fall In Love?

Don't keep it a secret...

Share "Woman In Love" with someone you know.

Friends
Classmates
Cousins
Neighbors
Youth Group

Please Print:
Name: _____
Address: _____
City: _____ State: _____ Zip: _____
Phone: _____ E-mail: _____

Small Orders

Woman In Love.....................Quantity ___ x $12.95 = _____
Mother's Companion................ Quantity ___ x 9.95 = _____
Shipping..........................Quantity ___ x $2.95 = _____

Bulk Orders (10 or more)

Woman In Love.....................Quantity ___ x $10.00 = _____
Shipping Total on all bulk orders.................................. = $12.00

Calculate Total.. = _____

Send this form and check
payable to:

Hearts United, Inc.
PO Box 6947
Katy, TX 77491

For fastest delivery:

Make orders online at

www.womaninlove.org

Made in the USA
Lexington, KY
24 August 2019